THE EDITORS OF *READER'S DIGEST*

WORD POWER

An Anthology of Articles & Tests

with an Introduction by Peter Funk

A BERKLEY/READER'S DIGEST BOOK
published by
BERKLEY BOOKS, NEW YORK

WORD POWER

A Berkley/Reader's Digest Book, published by arrangement with Reader's Digest Press

PRINTING HISTORY
Berkley/Reader's Digest edition/November 1980

Grateful acknowledgment is made to the following organizations and individuals for permission to reprint material from the indicated sources:

Mr. Clifton Fadiman for "Plain Thoughts on Fancy Language" and "I Know Whatcha Mean"; Farrar Straus & Giroux, Inc. for "A Word With You, Miss Thistlebottom," condensed from MISS THISTLEBOTTOM'S HOBGOBLINS: THE CAREFUL WRITER'S GUIDE TO THE TABOOS, BUGBEARS AND OUTMODED RULES by Theodore M. Bernstein, copyright © 1971 by Theodore M. Bernstein; The Christian Science Monitor for "Like, I Mean, You Know, Right?" by Roderick Nordell, copyright © 1972 by The Christian Science Publishing Society; Viking Penguin Inc. for "Classroom Classics"; Farrar Straus condensed from BIGGER AND BETTER BONERS, edited by Alexander Abingdon, copyright © 1952 by The Viking Press and reprinted by permission of Viking Penguin Inc.; Harper & Row, Publishers, Inc. for "Write The Way You Talk" condensed from SAY WHAT YOU MEAN by Rudolf Flesch, copyright © 1972 by Rudolf Flesch and reprinted by permission of Harper & Row, Publishers, Inc.; The Bobbs-Merrill Company, Inc. for "A Civil Tongue" condensed from A CIVIL TONGUE by Edwin Newman, copyright © 1975, 1976 by Edwin Newman; The Columbia Forum for "Was Paul Revere a Minuteperson?" by Jacques Barzun, copyright © 1974 by The Trustees of Columbia University in the City of New York; Channel Press/Hawthorn Books Inc. for "Watch Your Language!" condensed from MORE LANGUAGE THAT NEEDS WATCHING by Theodore M. Bernstein, copyright © 1962 by Theodore M. Bernstein; Mr. Stuart Chase for "How To Argue", "A Tip on Straight Thinking" and "Neither Black Nor White"; San Francisco Examiner for "Thank You, William Shakespeare!" by Guy Wright, copyright © 1964 by The News Call Bulletin; Crown Publishers, Inc. for "Alphabet You'll Like These Puns" by John S. Crosbie, condensed from CROSBIE'S DICTIONARY OF PUNS, copyright © 1977 by John S. Crosbie; Newsweek (May 6, 1968) for "Anything Goes, Verbalizationwise", copyright © 1968 by Newsweek, Inc.; Mrs. James Thurber for "The Meaning Manglers" by James Thurber. Copyright © 1960 James

Contents

INTRODUCTION

The Wonder of Words

BY PETER FUNK

Though you may not be aware of it consciously, the fact is you have always had an interest in language. The day you were born you attempted to express your feelings and you've been trying to do so ever since.

As you grew older the sounds you made developed into definite forms or words which were symbols representing your thoughts. At three you were able to use at least 1000 words and understood three or four thousand more. By ten your vocabulary had increased dramatically to perhaps as many as 20,000 words.

During this period you were discovering how to put these words together to make sense. With some difficulty you learned to write and to memorize the various peculiarities of spelling. You were taught to read and you found out writers could use words as weapons, as humor, to instruct or to create emotions. You began to understand also that like it or not the way each of us uses our words determines to some degree how others rate us.

1

At times you probably wanted to know more about language, to build your vocabulary, to write and speak well.

Word Power answers these needs. The book grew out of articles that have appeared in *Reader's Digest* and selections of my monthly "Word Power" feature.

At one time "It Pays to Enrich Your Word Power"® used the word "increase" rather than "enrich." DeWitt Wallace, founder of the *Digest* suggested the change.

"Increase" means to become greater in size, amount, degree, and the like—a straightforward word, plain and simple.

"Enrich" is another kind of word altogether. It suggests depth, wealth, abundance and profusion. There is a grandeur and promise to the word.

There is a grandeur and promise too for you in this book. It is a splendid compilation of information—learned, interesting, entertaining, humorous and useful. You can read it for enjoyment, play the vocabulary tests as a game and at the same time you will be absorbing knowledge that will enrich your entire life.

What excites me is the scope and the superb quality of WORD POWER. It covers virtually every aspect of our language from history to usage, giving you a purview no other existing book can match. The editors culled through past issues of the *Digest* selecting nearly 50 articles, many written by eminent authorities and well-known authors, such as: James Thurber, Jacques Barzun, Theodore M. Bernstein, Corey Ford, Clifton Fadiman, Stuart Chase, Edwin Newman, Fulton Oursler, Cornelia Otis Skinner, Dr. Haim G. Ginott and many others.

The articles range from topics such as the ancient legacy of our words to the fact that the ones we use are fingerprints of our thoughts and attitudes. We learn how to write business letters, speak to children, recognize illogical talk, listen intelligently and to avoid verbal booby traps. A glance at the table of contents suggests the unusual range of material.

The "Word Power" tests are interspersed among the various articles. Take them at your leisure. You may find it worthwhile to keep a record of the words that give you difficulty and from time to time review them.

Why is a good working vocabulary such a definite asset to have? The answer is that we think with words. We read, we study, we understand, we write with them. You and I may have a "feeling" or an amorphous idea or a vague sense about something. But it will not become a clearly defined image unless we become a kind of sculptor.

A sculptor shapes his feeling or idea by molding clay until the image he has in mind emerges. We, as sculptors of ideas, mold a possible thought into what is clear and understandable by using the right words.

Johnson O'Connor, a pioneer in the study of vocabulary ratings, observed that "although it is impossible to define success rigidly, a large vocabulary seems to be typical of all successful persons."

Before George Gallup founded the famous Gallup polls, he was a college teacher who especially stressed vocabulary growth among his students. He told me: "Whenever someone questions the value of vocabulary development, I point out that words are the tools of thought. The more extensive and precise a student's vocabulary, the more exact the student's thinking. Undoubtedly this explains why there is such a high correlation between the results of vocabulary tests and intelligence tests."

In his review of the book *The Children of the Counter-culture*, Anatole Broyard makes the electrifying statement that "the authors demonstrate an anemic vocabulary can be even more damaging than an unhealthy diet."

As I perused the material in *Word Power* I kept thinking of my father, Wilfred Funk. As a lexicographer and poet, he had a lifelong love affair with words. Like most people in love he was bursting to tell everyone about it. An interesting word thrilled him just as a spectacular scene moves an artist, or a concept captivates a scientist. In a group of people he could scarcely wait to tell about the intriguing etymology of a word he had just come across or about one of the delightful curiosities of the English language. He believed if he could only reach the public, millions of people would share his enthusiasm for the wonder and fascination of words. He was right, of course. Millions of copies of his books were sold and today are still best sellers in their field. "It Pays to Enrich Your World Power"® created by him in 1945 is one of the most popular features in *Reader's Digest*.

Here is a book he would have appreciated. Varied and rich in content, written by people who also have a love for words, one that explores the wonders of our language as well as showing us how to get the best use out of it.

To ask about the meaning of words is to ask about everything. To use them with skill and integrity is to become a master of expression. May *Word Power* encourage you on this path.

Words—Our Most Ancient Legacy

Next time you count, or speak of your brother or sister, you are using heirlooms thousands of years old

BY W. L. WHITE

What are your oldest heirlooms? Not Great-Grandfather's Civil War cavalry saber. Not even Great-Great-Grandmother's wedding silver. They are words you use for familiar things—water, corn, sun, moon, father, mother. These heirloom words—more ancient than the Pyramids, more enduring than the walls of Troy—have been handed down to us from a tiny, nameless and forgotten tribe which, five or six thousand years ago, was the ancestor of our speech.

Today, people of all races in Europe, India, South Africa, the Americas and the Pacific islands use almost these same words and many others like them. This makes us speech cousins to more than a billion people.

Scholars had long puzzled over the striking similarity of words in different languages. In Dutch, *vader;* in Latin, *pater;* in Swedish, *fader;* in German, *vater;* in Irish, *athir;* in Persian, *pidar;* in the Sanskrit of distant India, *pitr*. These words all sounded alike and meant the same thing—*father,* in English.

How did it happen that widely separated peoples used such closely related sound symbols? The problem baffled linguists for years, the more so because "father" was but one of a host of such "coincidences." Toward the end of the 18th century it dawned on scholars that perhaps all these words stemmed from some common language spoken far back before recorded history.

At last the brilliant German, Jacob Grimm, and other scholars of his time worked out a "law" of language changes. Their discoveries showed that the changes which take place during the history of a language are regular and consistent enough to permit comparisons between languages and to reconstruct the earlier stages of languages.

Once the law of change was clear, scholars could see that the many words for *father* all pointed back to an original, PATER; that *water* in English, *wasser* in German, *hydor* in Greek, *voda* in Russian (vodka is "little water"), *udan* in Sanskrit, and even *watar* in the language of King David's captain, Uriah the Hittite—all could have come only from an original WODOR. Using the law, they could trace the origin of countless words.

The scholars evolved an entire ancient vocabulary. They labeled this early speech "Indo-European," because it had both Indic and European branches. There is a Latin branch, from which stem Italian, Spanish, Portuguese, French, Rumanian; there is a Germanic branch, which includes English, German, Danish, Dutch, Swedish, Norwegian; the Celtic branch includes Welsh, Irish, Breton; the Slavic includes Russian, Polish, Czech, Bulgar, Serb; in addition, Indo-European includes Lithuanian, Persian, Greek, Armenian and a score of dialects in India which have sprung from ancient Sanskrit.

What tribe first spoke that mother tongue which hatched out this brood of cousin languages?

Today we know much about these dawn people, even though archeologists have uncovered not a single crumbling wall, nor any fragment of pottery which we can be sure was theirs.

By years of work—comparing Sanskrit with Greek and Gothic with Latin, language students have reconstructed old Indo-European mother words just as a paleontologist puts together a long-extinct reptile from a hatful of bones. And with these old words as evidence, we can reconstruct that ancient civilization that existed perhaps six thousand years ago.

We find that the family unit may well have been as strong then as now, for English *brother* comes from their word BHRATER, as *sister* comes from their SWESOR, our word *son* from their SUNU. English *daughter* has close cousins: *dottir* in Icelandic, *doche* in Russian and, closest of all, *dukhtar* in distant Persia—all stemming from DHUGHATER.

In culture the Indo-Europeans were far ahead of the North American Indians, who had no domestic animals except dogs. Our speech ancestors had domesticated the cow (GWOU), which gave them milk (MELG). From this strain they also bred oxen (UKSEN), which were joined together with a yoke (YUG). What did they pull? Surely a *wagon,* for this word comes from their WEGH (meaning "to carry")— and doubly surely because we know they had the wheel (QEQLO), a wondrous device that was unknown in the primitive Americas until Columbus.

They also knew sheep (their own became English *ewe*), which surely were tame, for from their fleece (PLEUS) they got wool (WLANA), which they had learned to weave (WEBH) into cloth and then sew (SIW) into garments.

Their old word for dog was KUN, which came into English as *hound,* into Latin as *canis,* then crossed back into English as *canine*. (Cats were unknown and, since the Arabs called them *qitt* and the Turks *kedi* [maybe our kitty?], it is probably that this dwarf tiger crept late into our homes from some Asian or African jungle, and its name from another speech family.) They also knew the pig (SU—English *sow* and *swine*) and the horse (EKWO—Latin *equus,* into English *eques*trian).

We might think of these ancestors as only wandering nomads had we not found their word for plow, which was ARA. Because of Latin *arare* (to plow), we speak in English of land which is *arable*—which can be cultivated.

What did they plant? Their word GRANO gives English *grain.* Of this GRANO, one kind they planted may have been light in color, for their word for *white* (KWEIT), coming down through Old Germanic *hweits*, then gave us English *wheat*.

Corn points to permanent settlements in which each family has a home. They called it a DOM, and from this old word Latin got *domus* and then gave us *domicile, domestic* and *dome*. Was this ancient DOM a rude tent of skins? We can be sure not, for DOM gave us English *tim*ber, of which their homes were built. How was this timber cut? Certainly with an AKS, which was probably of flint, for this Late Stone Age people knew little of metals, but called them all by a common word from which we have derived *iron*.

These speech ancestors of ours ground their grain in a mill (MEL), added water and yeast (YES) to make a dough (DHEIGH), which they would bake (BHOG) in an oven (UQNO) to make bread (PA—Latin *panis*, hence English *pantry*, the place where bread is kept).

All this we know from those old root words, which have come down to us in a score of languages. Likewise their numerals, which were: 1, OINOS; 2, DUO; 3, TREIES; 4, QETWER; 5, PENQE; 6, SWEKS; 7, SEPTN; 8, OKTO; 9, NEWN; 10, DEKM.

While each modern language has changed them, at least half the list would be understood by a native of ancient Greece, or by a modern native of London, Moscow, Bombay or Buenos Aires.

Had these people a government? Their word meaning "to rule" was REG, from which India got *rajah*, Latin got *rex*. "To lead" was DEUK, which has changed to *tug* in English.

Where did these ancestors of ours live? Since all Indo-European languages lack a common word for lion, tiger, elephant, camel or palm, the homeland could not have been far south. Their old word SNEIGHW (English *snow*, Russian *sneig*, Greek *nipha*, Welsh *nyf*, Latin *nix*, French *neige*) might even push this homeland far northward.

Wild animals we know they knew are the snake (SERP), the beaver (BHEBHRU), the bear, the goose, the rabbit and the duck. They had a word for small streams (STREW), and another for little ponds, which came down into English as *marsh*, *mire* and *moor*, and into Latin as *mare*—hence

English *mariner* and *maritime*. But of vast salt oceans they probably knew nothing: when, fanning out, migrating branches of the tribe met the thunder of ocean surf, each gave to this new marvel a separate name.

Of trees, they knew the birch and the beech and because, much later, the writings of North Europe were scratched on smooth beech boards, we get our English word *book*.

Biologists point out that all these animals and trees are natives of the temperate zone. Many other signs point to one possible location in Central Europe, which has roughly the boundaries of the old Austrian Empire.

Gradually, pushed by overpopulation or invaders, the "Indo-Europeans" began to move. The wanderings lasted thousands of years and led them far afield. One branch was to push Slavic up to the polar sea, another was to bring Latin down to the Meditteranean, while still others were to carry Celtic into what is today England and France, and Germanic down to the Rhine's right bank and up into Scandinavia.

We have inherited a rich legacy, one that ties us to many nations. There is yet one more item: our English word God comes from ancient GHUTOM, meaning "the Being that is worshiped." The syllable SAC meant *sac*red, then as now. From PREK (to pray) down through Latin *precari* (to pray) comes our word *prayer*.

Be sure that these Indo-European speech ancestors of ours must have pondered the dim mysteries of their own beginnings, even as do you (YU)!

Our Native Tongue, Alive and Well

Despite some lunatic lunges into pomposity, jargon and fads, American English is really just growing up

BY RODERICK MACLEISH

"Just got some new skins," says one teen-ager to another in a New York suburb.

"Lotsa bread?" asks his friend.

"Like nothing, man, nothing."

"I dig."

Meanwhile, in a recent election campaign, a gubernatorial candidate in an Eastern state complained of his opponent, "He circumvents the desirability of meaningful confrontation-type interaction by refusing to talk to me in this regard media-wise."

Believe it or not, these people are speaking the same language, or at least two dialects of the same language—commonly known as American English. The teen-ager was telling his friend that he had got a bargain on a set of drums. The gubernatorial candidate was explaining his inability to entice his adversary into a television debate.

Whether Americans like these are speaking English *correctly* is a question that has had teachers, linguists, editors, writers and other experts on our language at one another's throats. Often such authorities denounce some of the commonest words and phrases in current use. I disagree. I think that our language is actually in rather good shape. It just happens to be going through several absurd-sounding phases at the same time. But this should hardly trigger alarm. For it is just another in a long series of lunges into the unorthodox that have kept American English the marvelous, unpredictable, zany and utterly useful language it is.

Americans have always mauled, twisted, improvised upon and innovated in the language they brought from England.* The first settlers did it because they *had* to. Confronted with birds, animals and landscapes for which there were no English names, they took terms directly from American Indian languages—hickory, chipmunk, pecan, hominy, raccoon, skunk, moose, opossum, caribou, squash. At the same time, Indian expressions were translated into English. The first Euro-Americans referred to themselves as "palefaces," talked of "going on the warpath" and "burying the hatchet."

The next expansion of American English came with the waves of immigrants to the New World. From Mexican Spanish came the words chocolate, tomato and avocado. Dutch settlers contributed boss, cookie and spook, while German-Americans gave us sauerkraut, noodle and so on.

By the beginning of the 19th century, a whole new spoken dialect had emerged—reflecting Americans' westward, wilderness-taming, melting-pot experience. If in 1800 an American had told an Englishman that he had cleared the *underbrush,* built a *log cabin* in the *backwoods* and breakfasted on *johnnycake* before hunting *muskrats* and *bullfrogs* down near the *rapids,* the Englishman wouldn't have had the slightest idea of what his American friend was talking about.

American parents in the 1920s were equally bewildered when their jazz-age kids erupted with expressions such as "That's the cat's pajamas" and "Oh, you kid!" The jazz-

*More than 300 million people use English as their first language today, scattered across the world in a pattern originally given shape by the British Empire. Inevitably, these people of separate cultures have rearranged the one million words of the English language to suit their own needs.

agers were in turn nonplused when their children began shrieking, "Hey Ba-Ba Re-Bop!" and "Beat me Daddy, eight to the bar." And today's parents gape when their shaggy youngsters come forth with "Just got new skins." Yet such fanciful flights away from the loose standards of American English all convey a good deal of insight about us individually and as a nation.

The kids of the '20s were celebrating society's breakout from smothering 19th-century formality: jazz music was as good a symbol as any of the new emancipation. The smash-bang language of the 1940s signaled a joyful recovery from the Depression (itself immortalized in terms like "bread line," and "the crash"). Today young white Americans are adopting, wholesale, the language of black America. In the process they are telling us that they identify and sympathize with the struggle of black America to find its deserved place in our society.

Meanwhile, some wonderfully articulate phrases are swirling into our language. What better describes the tension we all experience than the phrase "up tight"? We had no precise word for lively, direct communication until "rapping" appeared. If something is simply too splendid to describe, it is, truly, "out of sight," as today's kids tell us, and when several people leave a group, they are, literally, "splitting." (Black English is itself in evolution. "Funky"— a word quite popular with today's young—used to mean smoky or smelly. Now it means down-to-earth or real. "Cop-out" originally meant to be arrested. Now it says that you are disassociating yourself from something.)

Those of us over 30 tend to be irritated when we hear our children stringing all of this together in a juvenile idiom. That's natural: anybody is jumpy when surrounded by people speaking a language he doesn't fully understand. But just in case we become a little smug in the belief that *we* are speaking normal, ordinary American English, here's news for you. Millions of us are developing a decidedly unusual language fad of our own. In the last 25 or so years, we have begun to speak a sort of written English, whose basic purposes are to sound cultivated and to soften the impact of what we say.

The faintly stilted talk of telephone operators; the airline stewardess who says, "If you wish to purchase a beverage, please indicate your selection on the form . . ."; the stiff, dehumanized jargon of some radio and television announcers—all are examples of this textbook tendency. Unfortunately, it has nearly run amok (and *that*, in case you're interested, is almost the only Malay word in the English language).

Some warm, human words are vanishing from daily talk, replaced by their written alternatives. "People" has become "persons," for example. When someone says, "Eight persons were given awards," it sounds more like a statistical report than an event. "Home" has replaced "house." The guy who constructs them is now called a "home builder." (I fearfully await the day when Rover's backyard shed becomes a "dog home.")

According to Jacques Barzun, of Columbia University, part of this new language fad can be traced to the influence of science and technology. They have been pouring such a torrent of new words and phrases into English that we have decided that each new thing should have an elegant new name. This has created what Barzun calls our "passion for jargon." Thus, the garbageman has become a "sanitation engineer," and the kid who isn't doing well in school—that kid who used to be called dumb, lazy or troubled—is now an "underachiever." Cemeteries have become "memorial parks," prisons "houses of detention" and slums "the inner city." Whatever events and conditions might be offensive we now sensitively try to disguise. (Yet a rose by any name is still a rose. One 84-year-old friend of mine blew up recently when someone applied a new euphemism to him. "Damn it!" he roared, "I'm *not* a senior citizen! *I am an old man!*")

None of the interesting and far-out things Americans are doing to their language really matter as long as we get the message across to each other, argues one school of linguists. As State Department linguist James Bostain puts it, if you can be understood, if you project the social image that you want to, you are speaking correctly. Counters another school: There *is* such a thing as proper English, and we should all try to achieve it. Language specialist Elizabeth Stone says, "There appears to be a prevalent notion in the

United States today that to be accepted in certain groups one must watch one's speech to see that it isn't too good." She does not go as far as President John Adams, who fancied the setting up of an Academy of American English, but she does call for a national effort to improve our language.

Still, to me, the messages pulsating out of the various gyrations of current American English are, on the whole, promising. If our young are displaying a personal sympathy with the cause of equality, if older people are developing a greater sensitivity to one another's feelings, if technology is enriching our vocabulary (and, by implication, our thinking and our vision), then the sometimes baffling, sometimes unorthodox and sometimes strikingly original ways we speak are optimistic signals. If, in the process, we engage in some jawbreaking gobbledygook, no great harm is done.

For all of its oddities, American English is, without doubt, increasingly influential around the world. To all of us persons in our homes, that is out of sight news, man—out of sight.

Word Power Test No. 1

Words of Lincoln

BY PETER FUNK

Abraham Lincoln, who spoke and wrote with consummate grace and wit, put special stress on precision. The following 20 words have been selected from his speeches and letters. How many of them can you define correctly? Check the word or phrase you believe is *nearest in meaning* to the key word. Answers appear at the end of the test.

1. **consecrate** (kon′ se krāt)—A: to bury. B: beautify. C: sanctify. D: shock.

2. **paramount** (păr′ ă mount)—A: supreme. B: urgent. C: large. D: valuable.

3. **alloy** (al′ oy)—whatever A: calms. B: warns. C: impairs. D: aids.

4. **munificence** (mū nĭf′ ĭ sense)—A: lavish generosity. B: courtesy. C: elegance. D: nobility of attitude.

5. **judicious** (ju dish′ us)—A: wise. B: suitable. C: tactful. D: shrewd.

6. **trifling** (trī′ fling)—A: foolish. B: insignificant. C: ridiculous. D: irrelevant.

7. **controvert** (kon′ truh vert)—A: to modify. B: be logical. C: dissuade. D: dispute.

8. **secede** (sē sēd′)—A: to relinquish. B: withdraw. C: give up. D: follow.

9. **unrequited** (un re quĭt′ ed)—A: not reciprocated. B: unnecessary. C: hopeless. D: unanswered.

10. **malice** (mal′ is)—A: sarcasm. B: bitterness. C: ill will. D: evil.

11. **insinuation** (in sin ū ā′ shun)—A: accusation. B: hint. C: claim. D: falsification.

12. **breach** (brēch)—A: reinforcement. B: secret. C: difficulty. D: opening.

13. **perpetuity** (pur pĕ tū′ ĭ tē)—A: eternity. B: durability. C: resilience. D: boredom.

14. **coercion** (kō er′ shun)—A: trick. B: plea. C: pressure. D: temptation.

15. **misconstrue** (mis con strōō′)—A: to destroy. B: disfigure. C: misinterpret. D: complicate.

16. **despotism** (dĕs′ pō tiz′m)—A: cruelty. B: tyranny. C: inflexibility. D: destruction.

17. **ascertain** (as er tān′)—A: to question. B: reveal. C: approve. D: determine.

18. **supersede** (sū per sēd′)—A: to achieve success. B: go before. C: add to. D: replace.

19. **assiduously** (as sĭd′ ū us lē)—A: diligently. B: scathingly. C: enthusiastically. D: helpfully.

20. **entwine**—A: to enchant. B: tie. C: attach. D: interweave.

ANSWERS

1. **consecrate**—C: To sanctify; set apart as sacred; as, "In a larger sense we cannot...*consecrate*...this ground," Lincoln declared at Gettysburg. Latin *consecrare* (to make holy).

2. **paramount**—A: Supreme; chief; the most important; as, "My *paramount* objective is to save the Union." Old French *par* (by) and *amont* (above).

3. **alloy**—C: Whatever impairs or reduces the purity of; as, "They make no pretense of loving liberty and do not have the base *alloy* of hypocrisy." Old French *aloi* (mixture).

4. **munificence**—A: Lavish generosity; as, "making known your *munificence* and kind consideration." Latin *munificus* (generous, liberal).

5. **judicious**—A: Wise; prudent; as, "your very patriotic and *judicious* letter." Latin *judicium* (judgment).

6. **trifling**—B: Insignificant; so trivial as to be negligible; as, "In some *trifling* particulars the condition of the race has been ameliorated." Middle French *trufle* (deception).

7. **controvert**—D: To dispute; argue against; contradict or deny; as, "It was intended to *controvert* opinions." Latin *controvertere* (to turn against).

8. **secede**—B: To withdraw from membership in a federation; quit; as, "If one state may *secede*, so may another." Latin *secedere* (to go away).

9. **unrequited**—A: Not reciprocated; not compensated for; not

returned in kind; as, "250 years of *unrequited* toil." Old English *un-* (not), and English *requite* (to make return for).

10. **malice**—C: Active ill will; desire to make others suffer; as, "with *malice* toward none." Latin *malus* (bad).

11. **insinuation**—B: A hint; implication; subtle, indirect suggestion; as, "Your *insinuations* of unfairness on my part are unjust." Latin *insinuare* (to introduce by windings or turnings).

12. **breach**—D: An opening or hole as when a wall is broken through. Therefore, a situation calling for urgent action; as, "to throw myself into the *breach*." Old French *breche*.

13. **perpetuity**—A: Eternity; the quality of lasting indefinitely or being perpetual; as, "*Perpetuity* is implied in the fundamental law of all national governments." Latin *perpetuus*.

14. **coercion**—C: Pressure; the application of force, as by threats or intimidation; as, "Would it be *coercion* also if the state was forced to submit?" Latin *coercere* (to enclose, shut in).

15. **misconstrue**—C: To misinterpret; as, "Judge Campbell *misconstrues*." Middle English *mis-* (mistaken) and *construen* (construe).

16. **despotism**—B: Tyranny; as, "When a man governs himself, and also governs another man, that is more than self-government—that is *despotism*." French *despotisme*.

17. **ascertain**—D: To determine by experiment, inquiry, etc.; as, "if we *ascertain* what we differ about." Middle French *acertainer*.

18. **supersede**—D: Replace; supplant by being newer, better or more effective; as, "Judge Douglas has seen himself *superseded* in a Presidential nomination." Latin *supersedere* (to sit above).

19. **assiduously**—A: Diligently; as, "I practiced law more *assiduously* than ever before." Latin *assiduus* (always sitting near; hence, attentive).

20. **entwine**—D: To interweave; as, "the principle of 'liberty to all,' *entwining* itself more closely about the human heart." Middle English *en-* (in) and *twynen* (double or twisted thread).

VOCABULARY RATINGS

20—18 correct ....exceptional
17—15 correct ....excellent
14—12 correct .... good

Your Words
Give You Away

For a better understanding of yourself and others, try
listening "between the lines"

BY JOHN KORD LAGEMANN

After a visit from a friend, my mother would review the
conversation in her mind, the pauses, inflections and choice
of words, then announce the real news the caller never
mentioned: "Henry wants to sell his house." "Frank is going
to marry Janie." "Young Mrs. Cole thinks she's pregnant
but isn't sure."

Mother was no mind reader, she was practicing a technique we now call "content analysis." It's a kind of systematic search for the small verbal clues that, when put
together, reveal a larger meaning: attitudes, intentions, behavior patterns, underlying strategy. As Ben Jonson wrote
more than 300 years ago, "Language springs out of the
inmost parts of us. No glass renders a man's likeness so
true as his speech."

Experts in business and science use highly developed
content-analysis techniques to measure changes in consumer attitudes and to diagnose emotional conflicts. Governments keep corps of analysts monitoring other nations'

broadcasts and printed materials to extract useful intelligence. Details that seem trivial by themselves have a way of adding up, when classified and counted, to vital information. I've found—as have many other people—that certain tricks of content analysis help you to read between the lines of ordinary conversation.

FINGERPRINT WORDS. A word or group of words that recurs frequently is one of the surest clues to who or what is on a person's mind. As any parent knows, you can easily tell which of your daughter's boy friends is becoming the new favorite—sometimes before the girl herself is really aware of it—simply by counting the number of times the name is mentioned.

But the technique can have more subtle applications. For example, verbal fingerprinting helped a young lawyer handle a difficult client with whom other members of the firm had been unable to get along. The young man collected all letters and memos from the client in his firm's files. As he read them he was struck by recurrent expressions and allusions typical of a certain period of English literature. Further investigation revealed the client as a prodigiously well-read amateur scholar, a shy man who hid his sensitivity behind a cantankerous manner. With this key to the client's personality, the lawyer had no trouble in gaining his confidence.

THE BIG PRONOUN. We instinctively notice how often someone says, "I," "me," "my" and "mine." To most of us, excessive use of the first person singular simply means that the person is a bore—but it can mean something more. "When one's automobile is out of order," says Dr. O. Hobart Mowrer of the University of Illinois, "one is likely to refer to it oftener. Likewise, when a person's psychic equipment is grating and squeaking, it is understandable that his attention should be directed toward it much of the time."

Counts made at the University of Iowa and the University of Cincinnati demonstrate that hospitalized mental patients use "I" oftener than any other word—about once every 12 words, three times as often as normal people. As these patients recover, their use of "I" and "they" goes down, and their use of "we" goes up.

THE JUDGMENT TEST. One way of recognizing a person's values is by cataloguing the particular adjectives he uses to express approval and disapproval. With one of my friends the fundamental criterion is practicality: good things he describes as "feasible," "applicable," "functional"; things he doesn't like are "unworkable."

Several years ago a close friend of ours became engaged to a man whose usual words of praise were "powerful," "strong," "overwhelming." Things he disliked were "weak," "tiny" or "insignificant." He seemed to judge everything on the basis of size and power. Our friend, on the other hand, was a woman of artistic interests whose value judgments were mainly in terms of "beautiful" versus "ugly." It was no great surprise when they found they "did not see eye to eye," and broke the engagement.

IMAGES AND THEMES. The metaphors, similes and analogies a person uses not only reflect his life experience but tell you how he thinks. Individuals have certain dominant themes, highly revealing of character. One man I know constantly uses images that suggest he is steering toward a distant landfall through buffeting winds. His main concern is to "keep his bearings" and "stay on course." He urges friends to "state their position" and to be sure they "know where they are going." A nautical background is indicated—but, more than that, a whole philosophy of life.

HOW DO YOU FEEL? Psychologists Dr. John Dollard of Yale and Dr. Mowrer devised a sort of emotional barometer by comparing the number of words a person uses expressing discomfort of any kind—ill health, annoyance or boredom—with the number of words which express relief, comfort, fun or satisfaction. They use this "Discomfort-Relief Quotient" to measure progress in the emotional adjustment of a patient undergoing treatment. If in the course of a few minutes' casual conversation a man has used no comfort words at all but has mentioned the "horrible" weather, the "appalling" headlines, the "dull" plays being written these days and the "aggravating" traffic situation, he doesn't have to add that he is feeling out of tune with the world.

A similar formula was developed by Dr. Harold Lasswell of the Yale School of Law. He counted the number of favorable self-references in a person's speech and the number of self-derogatory references, and used the ratio as a measure of self-esteem. Dr. Lasswell also counted the favorable and unfavorable references to others. Comparing the two sets, he found that the person with high self-esteem tends to be well disposed toward others, too.

GRAMMAR COUNTS. Verb tenses can provide a hint as to how much a person dwells in the past as compared with his concern for the present and his plans and hopes for the future. When the past tense predominates it may indicate melancholy or depression.

Passive versus active is another clue. A decided preference for passive constructions—"I found myself there" instead of "I went there"—may reflect a feeling of impotence, active constructions a sense of power and responsibility.

ER . . . AH. . . . A doctor friend told me recently that in taking the history of a new patient he sometimes learns as much from the hesitations as from the direct answers. "Occupation?" The person who's happy with his job usually answers promptly. A long pause, a cough, laugh, throat clearing or sniffle may indicate trouble in that department. "Married or single?" Again, in this doctor's experience, a hesitation can be meaningful.

Pauses may indicate tension or anxiety associated with the words that follow. "I, er, ah, love you" means something very different from a forthright "I love you."

Using clues like these, my friends and I have gained a surer understanding of one another, and even of ourselves. Content analysis will never replace reason or common sense, of course. But it can supplement them, and sometimes reveal messages we would otherwise miss completely.

Are You a Skid-Talker?

BY COREY FORD

"You can't blame me for making a mistake," my friend Bunny said the other day. "After all, none of us are human." I was trying to figure that one out when she added thoughtfully, "I may be wrong but I'm not far from it."

Bunny is a skid-talker. Skid-talk is more than a slip of the tongue. It's a slip of the whole mind. In effect, it puts one idea on top of another, producing a sort of mental double exposure—and my friend Bunny is a master of the art. When her husband, a prominent Hollywood director, completed a screen epic recently she told him loyally, "I hope it goes over with a crash." She was very enthusiastic after the preview. "It's a great picture," she assured everyone. "Don't miss it if you can."

That's the insidious thing about skid-talk—you're never quite sure you've heard it. Skid-language is like a time bomb; it ticks away quietly in your subconscious, and suddenly, a few minutes later, your mind explodes with the abrupt realization that something about the remark you just heard was a trifle askew.

"If George Washington were alive today," Bunny told me once, "he'd turn over in his grave." On another occasion she opened a debate with the challenging sentence, "For your information, let me ask you a question."

The simplest kind of skid-talk consists of mixing words. For example:

"Too many cooks in the soup."

"From time immoral."

"There I was, left holding the jackpot."

"It was so dark you couldn't see your face in front of you."

"I want some hot-water juice and a lemon."

A devoted mother added another gem to my collection: "I'm going to have a bust made of my daughter's head." And a stranger whom I discovered feeding pigeons in Central Park explained to me with quiet dignity: "I believe in being dumb to kind animals."

Sometimes a skid-talker will turn an entire sentence inside out so effectively that the listener can't possibly set it straight again. I keep wondering about a statement I overheard the other day at the station: "He tells me something one morning and out the other." And I have yet to discover what's wrong with Bunny's advice to a young married couple: "Two can live as cheaply as one, but it costs them twice as much."

Bunny is a natural skid-zophrenic. "I'm a split personality all in one," she describes herself happily. She lives in a handsome country place of which she says dreamily, "Isn't it pretty? The lake comes right up to the shore." "I went to a wonderful party," she said of a recent celebrity-studded banquet. "Everybody in the room was there." She made sure to thank the hostess as she departed. "Darling, that was the best dinner I ever put in my whole mouth."

Bunny's insults are equally bewildering. "I never liked you, and I always will," she told a prominent screen star frankly. And a perennially young starlet is still trying to decipher Bunny's candid appraisal, "You're old enough to be my daughter."

The best skid-talk fuses two thoughts together, creating

a new shortcut which speeds up the language. I remember a New Year's Eve party when Bunny became fearful that the sounds of midnight revelry might disturb the neighbors. "Don't make so much noise," she told the celebrants. "Remember, this isn't the only house we're in."

I had an affectionate note from Bunny recently. "Come see us again soon," she wrote. "We miss you almost as much as if you were here."

Word Power Test No. 2

Relics of Old English

BY PETER FUNK

The following one-syllable words are living echoes of the fascinating linguistic period from about 450 to 1150—the era of Old English. The pithy vigor of these old words reflects the character of the fierce Northern Europeans who braved hazardous seas intent on plundering and conquering. Their talk would have been spare and to the point, in the 20 test words below. Choose the word or phrase *nearest in meaning* to the key word. Answers appear at the end of the test.

1. **hone**—A: to mourn. B: hum. C: sharpen. D: whittle.
2. **hulk**—A: rotten tree stump. B: broken-down ship. C: pile of debris. D: tumble-down barn.
3. **saw**—A: remedy. B: witticism. C: reference point. D: proverb.
4. **wield** (wēld)—A: to finagle. B: support. C: force upon. D: exercise authority.
5. **bight** (bīt)—A: post. B: meadow. C: porch. D: bay.
6. **creed**—a statement of A: belief. B: confidence. C: proof. D: qualification.
7. **girth**—A: ornament. B: diameter. C: circumference. D: knot.
8. **crop**—A: to winnow. B: bundle. C: steal. D: cut short.
9. **bane**—A: ignominy. B: affliction. C: ruler. D: regimen.
10. **eke** (ēk)—A: to startle. B: fade. C: supplement. D: escape.
11. **gnash** (nash)—A: to rip. B: nibble. C: grind. D: grin.
12. **font**—A: statue. B: tower. C: pulpit. D: source.
13. **quell**—A: to tremble. B: suppress. C: hide. D: alter.

14. **faze**—A: to eliminate. B: disturb. C: blur. D: endanger.
15. **shank**—A: shin. B: joke. C: link. D: joint.
16. **doff**—A: to blunder. B: hitch. C: bow. D: take off.
17. **lore**—A: fascination. B: sentiment. C: knowledge. D: trap.
18. **grit**—A: biscuit. B: temper. C: spite. D: pluck.
19. **deft**—A: orderly. B: quirky. C: experienced. D: skillful.
20. **wreak**—A: to smell. B: soak. C: twist. D: inflict.

ANSWERS

1. **hone**—C: To sharpen; give an edge to; as, to *hone* a knife for carving meat. Old English *han* (a stone).

2. **hulk**—B: Broken-down ship; deserted wreck; now, anything unwieldy. Old English *hulc* (ship).

3. **saw**—D: Proverb; a familiar homely saying; as, "'A bird in the hand is worth two in the bush' is a *saw* we've all heard." Old English *sagu* (a saying).

4. **wield**—D: To exercise authority, power or influence; make full use of; as, to *wield* political power. Old English *wealdan* (have power over).

5. **bight**—D: Bay formed by a curve in a shoreline; loop in a rope. Old English *byht* (bend).

6. **creed**—A: Authoritative statement of belief; set of principles; doctrine; as, the Apostles' *Creed* in the Christian faith. Old English *creda* (I believe), from Latin *credo*.

7. **girth**—C: Circumference; distance around something; as, the enormous *girth* of a redwood tree. Also, a strap around a horse to secure a saddle. Middle English *gerth,* akin to Old English *gyrdan* (to encircle).

8. **crop**—D: To cut short; trim; as, "A printer *crops* the edge of a page." Old English *cropp* (top, usually of a plant).

9. **bane**—B: Affliction; cause of harm or worry; as, "Inflation is the *bane* of our times." Old English *bana* (murderer).

10. **eke**—C: To supplement by great effort; manage with difficulty; as, to *eke* out a living. Old English *eac* (increase).

11. **gnash**—C: To grind one's teeth in anger or distress. Related to obsolete *gnast,* an Old English adaptation of Old Norse *gnaist* (a gnashing of teeth).

12. **font**—D: Source; as, "Grandmother was a *font* of family history." Old English *font* (basin for baptismal water) from Latin *fons* (spring).

13. **quell**—B: To suppress; put down by force; as, to *quell* a child's fears. Old English *cwellan* (to kill).

14. **faze**—B: To disturb; upset. Generally used in a negative sense; as, not to be *fazed* by a problem. Old English *fesian* (put to flight).

15. **shank**—A: Shin; leg from knee to ankle. Old English *sceanca* (shin).

16. **doff**—D: To take off; as, clothing from the body; raise; as, to *doff* one's hat. Old English *don of* (remove).

17. **lore**—C: Knowledge; collection of facts and traditions about a subject; as, Joseph Conrad's vast *lore* of the sea. Old English *lar*.

18. **grit**—D: Pluck; unflinching courage or determination; as, "The girl had true *grit* in overcoming obstacles." The basic meaning is coarse sand, from Old English *greot*.

19. **deft**—D: Skillful or adroit; having a light, neat and sure touch; as, to hit a golf ball with a *deft* stroke. Old English *gedaefte* (mild, gentle).

20. **wreak**—D: To inflict vengeance or destruction on an enemy; to damage. Most frequently used in the phrase "to *wreak* havoc." Old English *wrecan* (revenge, drive out).

VOCABULARY RATINGS

20—19 correct ....exceptional
18—15 correct ....excellent
14—12 correct ....good

Plain Thoughts on Fancy Language

BY CLIFTON FADIMAN

Not long ago I bookwormed my way into a radio program that involved talking about a Greek classic. The small stint over, one of my associates, an eminent scholar, remarked with a grin, "Nice to make a fast buck."

Now, scholarship and the "fast buck" are not natural bedfellows and I found myself pondering the professor's casual use of the phrase. Would it have been possible 25 years ago? Probably not. Fifty years ago? Surely not.

Today, however, the once stout barrier between "correct" and colloquial speech has thinned to a gossamer membrane. Fresher, more picturesque than stiff-collar English, the experimental phrase often drives out the established one, to become in turn standard speech.

All of us view language as we view matter, as something to be manipulated into new, exciting, useful shapes. On the whole the results have been fine. But this national talent will sometimes go hog-wild. It's fun to play with words—but not at the cost of clear communication.

"What is fittest in language," writes Thomas Pyles in his *Words and Ways of American English*, "has a way of surviving, as *the real McCoy, highbrow, crook, haywire, panhandle, roughneck*. What is graceless or fraudulent or ponderously 'cute' ekes out a banal and colorless existence among the silly, the sentimental and the addlepated. . . ."

You and I have set working thousands of useful inventions, such as *baby-sitter, soap opera, build-up*. But we have also, by thoughtless parroting, put in circulation a certain amount of fraudulent new word-currency. Here's a list which we may divide into a few convenient categories:

SHEEP-TALK: Sheep-talk flows from a fear of using garden-variety English as against the latest fashionable substitute catch-phrase. I am talking sheep when every minor verbal encounter becomes a *hassle* or when I overexercise such trumpery jocosities as *unlaxed, what gives?, big deal, look-see, wha hoppen?* and *oh brother!*

THE ENFEEBLING INTENSIFIER: There can be no objection to the sound, honest American *okay*. Less honest, however, is the current rash of emphatic substitutes for *yes:* the jerky-brisk *definitely!*, the fake-commercial *it's a deal*, the tiresomely bright-eyed *you can say that again!*

Other enfeebling intensifiers that enjoy a high degree of dispensability include: *frankly, candidly, basically* and the epidemic *personally* as in "I personally found it very educational." The addition of *personally* does not remove from *I* its presumed flavor of egotism. It merely weakens the word and thickens the sentence.

THE LEARNED VULGARISM: Whenever people are short on ideas they tend to use long words. Today this disease has attacked us in a rather special form, as a consequence of the popularization of science. We gain assurance when we use *allergy* for dislike, *schizophrenia* for mental eccentricities, *philosophy* for any notion or opinion, *psychology* for any insight into mental process, *complex* to denote a strong interest, *compulsive* for what is merely habitual, and so on.

Writers with an imperfect scientific education, such as myself, are much given to the learned vulgarism.

EXECUTIVE ENGLISH: *Variety*, the show-business trade paper that has been responsible for a host of brilliant additions to the vernacular, recently printed what it asserted to be a memorandum circulated at one of the major television networks:

"You will recall that we've been firming up this problem for some time, and just in the nature of pitching up a few mashie shots to see if we come near the green, I'd like to express these angles:

"I think we should take a reading of the whole general situation to see if it is being spitballed correctly so that we can eventually wham it through for approval or disapproval as the case might be. We've got to live with this for a long time, and there are certain rock-bottom slants that we will have to try on for size."

William H. Whyte, Jr., calls this the businessman's rebellion against bureaucratic gobbledegook. It is a rich hash of metaphors drawn from sport (largely football), technology, run-of-mine clichés, newspaper columns and the jargon of "social scientists" and "social engineers." This "reverse gobbledegook," Mr. Whyte believes, enables the speaker to conceal—with dynamic emphasis—the fact that he has nothing to say, and imparts to him "an appearance of savviness and general know-how."

Synthetic, its "punch" a delusion, this new jargon illustrates a statement made as far back as 1838 by James Fenimore Cooper: "The common faults of American language are an ambition of effect, a want of simplicity and a turgid abuse of terms."

Of course I'm just thinking out loud, fellers, but that's the pitch. 'Bye now. Be good.

A Word
With You, Miss
Thistlebottom

BY THEODORE M. BERNSTEIN

You remember Miss Thistlebottom. She was the eighth-grade English teacher whose rules were supposed to make our speech and writing models of clarity. "Don't split infinitives," she scolded. "Say, 'I shall,' not 'I will.'" Was she right? Are the rules really so rigid? No, said Theodore M. Bernstein, who for 20 years was assistant managing editor of the New York Times.

"In your efforts to keep your pupils upright," he told Miss Thistlebottom *in his book,* Miss Thistlebottom's Hobgoblins, *"you have sometimes bound them into a strait-jacket. Now I would like to have some words with you."*

Here are a few of those words.

AS FOLLOWS. Some people insist that when a plural subject is involved, the phrase indicating a listing coming up must be "as follow" rather than "as follows." For example, "The provisions of the new tax bill are as follow." They are wrong. For centuries, the idiom has been "as follows," regardless of the number of the subject—presumably an ellipsis of "*as* is set forth in the listing that *follows* ." The "as follow" advocates are guilty of overrefinement, like the girl aspiring to social grace who tackles her olive with a fork.

BEST FOOT FORWARD. Anyone who heard his English teacher say that a person should use the superlative degree only when three or more things are being compared would have to conclude that the phrase "best foot forward" must refer to a dog, octopus or centipede. But no, it refers to a human being, and as ancient idiom it is all right. If you were to say, "Put your better foot forward," friends would start looking around for commitment papers.

CONTACT. As a verb meaning to communicate with, "contact" has drawn objections. But it is by no means unusual for a noun to be verbed. Moreover, the word is often useful either because it replaces a longer locution, such as "get in touch with," or because it is intentionally less specific than, say, "phone," "write" or "call on."

DIFFERENT FROM, DIFFERENT THAN. Teachers insist on "different from," and when the words are followed by a noun or pronoun there should be no deviation: "Women are different *from* men"; "Her body is different *from* mine." Exceptions are becoming acceptable, however, when what follows is a clause, expressed or elliptical, and the use of "different from" would be awkward: "The feeling of weightlessness affected him this time in a *different* way *than* ever before."

-ED. Is it a "four-engined plane" or a "four-engine plane"? A "teenaged girl" or a "teen-age girl"? In these examples, either form is correct, although that is not true of all such compounds. It is a matter of idiom. If there is anything approaching a rule, it is that a noun formed into an adjective describing an animate creature usually takes the "-ed." Thus we have a "left-handed man," a "yellow-bellied sapsucker," a "floppy-eared dog."

GRADUATED. Nitpickers hold that it is incorrect to say, "He graduated from college." They are wrong. A student can either "graduate from" or be "graduated by" a college. It depends on whether you are thinking of his achievement in completing his studies or the institution's magnanimity in admitting him to a degree. Actually, "graduated from" is now more common.

IT'S ME. If someone were to show an English teacher a picture of her class and ask her to pick out a certain boy, she would surely not say, "That's him in the center." She would say, "That's he in the center." But what about the first person pronoun? If someone asked her who was standing in the last row, might she not say, "That's me"? "It's me" is certainly gaining, at least in spoken language, although it is not altogether established.

ME, TOO. Your dinner partner says, "I'd like a brandy," and you chime in, "Me, too." Grammatically you are wrong, no matter how right you are in ordering brandy. You should use the nominative case so that your sentence, when filled out, would go, "I, too, would like a brandy," not "Me, too, would like a brandy." Let us acknowledge, however, that at least in spoken English "Me, too" is idiomatic and acceptable, whereas "I, too" is grammatical but fairly uncommon.

PEOPLE, PERSONS. Around the turn of the century, grammarians adjured writers not to use "people" for persons individually. Since then, "people" has gained greater latitude. The emphasis should still be on the connotation of individuality, however. If you write, "Fifty people were present," you are thinking of the group, but if you write, "Forty-nine *persons* were injured," you are thinking of 49 individuals. A general rule, at least in written language, might be: Use "people" for large groups presented in round numbers, "persons" for an exact or smaller number.

QUITE. Strictly speaking, "quite" means completely or positively. ("He was *quite* wrong"; "It is *quite* the thing to do.") Not quite so strictly speaking, "quite" is used to mean rather or somewhat ("It is *quite* foggy in London") and "quite a" is used to mean a substantial but not unlimited quantity ("*Quite* a number of dissenters were present"). These unstrictly-speaking meanings show every sign of thriving and becoming acceptable.

'ROUND. Forget the apostrophe. In addition to being a legitimate adjective and noun. "round" is a legitimate preposition and adverb. Therefore save space and write "the year round" and "we showed the visitors round." Needless to say, "around" is perfectly good, too.

SHALL, WILL. Our teachers drilled into us that to express simple futurity we should use "shall" in the first person and "will" in the second and third persons, whereas to express determination we should reverse that order. But we quickly forgot the formula. The facts of usage are that the distinction simply is not made, although "shall" occasionally crops up to lend a touch of formality.

SPLIT INFINITIVE. If we do not boggle at "He favors really getting to the bottom of it," why should we boggle at "He wants to really get to the bottom of it"? Reputable writers are now shaking off the shackles. Within the near future the split-infinitive bugaboo may be finally laid to rest.

THAT, WHO. A newspaper reader sometimes thinks he has caught the paper in an error when he reads, "As is true of many other individuals *that* the President has appointed . . ." "Since when," he will write, "is 'that' rather than 'who' permissible in referring to persons?" The answer is: since the language was in its infancy. The King James version of the Bible gave us many instances, such as "Blessed is the man *that* walketh not in the counsel of the ungodly." "That" can refer to either persons or things.

Any further questions, Miss Thistlebottom?

Word Power Test No. 3

Medical Terms

BY PETER FUNK

"I enjoy convalescence. It is the part that makes illness worthwhile," quipped playwright George Bernard Shaw. You in turn might enjoy testing yourself on the following medical words selected from *Reader's Digest*. Pick the word or phrase nearest in meaning to the test word. Answers appear at the end of this test.

1. **vascular** (vas′ kū lar)—related to A: slipperiness. B: blood vessels. C: smallness. D: desiccation.

2. **perforate** (pur′ fō rāt)—A: to pierce. B: bind. C: close. D: ooze.

3. **hypochondriac** (hī pō kŏn′ drē ăk)—one who is A: short-tempered. B: overactive. C: too anxious about health. D: always dissatisfied.

4. **comatose** (kō′ mă tōs)—A: expansive. B: fearful. C: unconscious. D: indifferent.

5. **platelet** (plāt′ let)—A: glass dish. B: name tag. C: medical dressing. D: clotting substance.

6. **diuretic** (dī ū rĕt′ ĭk)—substance that stimulates A: eyes. B: kidneys. C: extremities. D: lungs.

7. **malinger** (mă lin′ ger)—A: to shirk. B: disobey. C: decline. D: complain.

8. **rubella** (rōō bel′ uh)—A: a blush. B: emetic. C: herb. D: disease.

9. **vertigo** (vur′ tĭ gō)—A: paleness. B: fear of falling. C: dizziness. D: confusion.

10. **atrophy** (ă′ trō fē)—A: to harden. B: wither. C: freeze. D: join.

11. **dehydration** (dē hī drā′ shun)—A: loss of fluids. B: saturation. C: reduced pressure. D: equalization.

35

12. **therapeutic** (ther uh pū′ tĭk)—A: stimulating. B: strong. C: natural. **D**: curative.

13. **diagnostic** (dī ăg nŏs′ tĭk)—serving to A: illustrate. B: speculate. **C**: identify a disease. D: communicate.

14. **intravenous** (in tra vē′ nus)—pertaining to A: connective tissue. **B**: a vein. C: musculature. D: the heart.

15. **psychosomatic** (sī kō sō mă′ tĭk)—involving **A**: mind and body. B: extrasensory perception. C: hypnotic healing. D: body language.

16. **trauma** (trow′ muh)—**A**: shock. B: paralysis. C: blockage. D: outburst.

17. **obese** (ō bēs′)—A: docile. B: slim. **C**: stout. D: coarse.

18. **antibody** (an′ ti bŏd ē)—A: splinter group. B: gravitational influence. C: that which worsens. **D**: immunizing agent.

19. **toxic** (tŏk′ sĭk)—A: bitter. B: foul-smelling. C: remedial. **D**: poisonous.

20. **dilate** (dī′ lāt)—A: to spin. B: weaken. **C**: widen. D: push out.

ANSWERS

1. **vascular**—B: Related to the vessels in a body or plant that carry fluids such as blood, lymph, sap; as, to have a healthy *vascular* system. Latin *vas* (small vessel; dish).

2. **perforate**—A: To pierce; puncture; as, a *perforated* eardrum. Latin *perforare* (to bore through).

3. **hypochondriac**—C: One who is overly anxious about his health and frequently imagines he has various diseases. Greek *hypokhondrion* (area under the breastbone once believed to be the seat of melancholy).

4. **comatose**—C: Unconscious; as if in a coma or stupor; lethargic. Greek *koma* (deep sleep). "The patient remained in a *comatose* condition."

5. **platelet**—D: Small coin-shaped particle in the blood necessary for clotting. From *plate* and *-let* (small).

6. **diuretic**—B: Medicinal substance that stimulates kidneys to eliminate excess body water. Greek *diourin* from *dia* (through) and *ourein* (to urinate).

7. **malinger**—A: To shirk; pretend sickness to avoid work. French *malingre* (sickly).

8. **rubella**—D: A mild contagious disease affecting young

people; also called German measles. Latin *rubellus* (reddish).

9. **vertigo**—C: Dizziness; the sensation that one's surroundings are whirling about; mental bewilderment. Latin *vertere* (to turn).

10. **atrophy**—B: To wither; waste away. Greek *atrophos* (poorly nourished) from *a-* (not) and *trophe* (nourishment).

11. **dehydration**—A: Excessive loss of water from the body. Latin *de-* (from) and Greek *hydor* (water). "Long-distance runners may suffer *dehydration*."

12. **therapeutic**—D: Curative; having healing qualities. Greek *therapeuein* (to nurse).

13. **diagnostic**—C: Concerning the identification of disease; as, *diagnostic* procedures such as X rays or blood tests. Greek *diagignoskein* (to distinguish).

14. **intravenous**—B: Directly into a vein; as, *intravenous* feeding. Latin *intra* (within) and *venous*.

15. **psychosomatic**—A: Pertaining to a physical disorder caused by emotional stress. Greek *psyche* (mind) and *soma* (body).

16. **trauma**—A: Emotional shock producing a lasting mental effect; as, children undergoing the *trauma* of war. Greek *trauma* (wound).

17. **obese**—C: The Latin *obedere* (to devour) gives us our word for stout.

18. **antibody**—D: An immunizing agent produced by the body to fight off infections; as, *antibodies* stimulated by flu shots. Greek *anti* (against) and *body*.

19. **toxic**—D: Poisonous; destructive. Greek *toxikon* (poison).

20. **dilate**—C: To widen; make larger; expand; as, "The medicinal drops *dilate* the pupils of the eyes." Latin *dilatare* (spread out, enlarge).

VOCABULARY RATINGS

20—19 correct ....exceptional
18—15 correct ....excellent
14—12 correct .... good

Like, I Mean, You Know, Right?

Here are six words you can communicate better without

BY RODERICK NORDELL

If only everyone talked the way we do in my household. I mean . . . if only everyone . . . like . . . talked . . . you know . . . the way we do . . . right?

It would be so much . . . like . . . easier to . . . you know . . . understand . . . right? If the 16th paragraph of the federal . . . you know . . . income-tax instruction had said:

"If . . . like . . . you qualify as a . . . you know . . . Certain Married Individual Living Apart . . . right? . . . check Single box . . . I mean . . . on Line 1 as . . . like . . . your filing status . . . right? . . . unless you also qualify as Unmarried . . . you know . . . Head of Household. In that case . . . like . . . check the Unmarried Head of Household Box . . . right? . . . on Line 4."

Isn't it time for official language to catch up to this common tongue, to these six little words—like, I mean, you know, right?—which are taking the place of punctuation and meaning in certain American families? I speak in defiance of my wife, who . . . like . . . periodically tries to . . . you know . . . ban the persistent little fellows.

I mean . . . she has not been without . . . like . . . effect. Especially on the telephone, for some reason, I have begun to notice my "you know" frequency. Swallowing the phrase when I am aware of it in time, I wonder what the . . . you know . . . person at the other end of the line thinks is happening.

Should one blame one's children as carriers of the six little words? Certainly we are no match for them in imaginative placement and speed of delivery, for they score even with the difficult like-at-the-beginning-of-the-sentence play.

But their innovative usages would not take root if one were not weak, weak, weak. Notice how all these words are not assertive but defensive, apologetic, hedging. They don't sharpen statements but round them down. They can hardly be considered character-building.

In years past, the undefined "you know" was sometimes used to express the inexpressible between people who thought alike. Now it is a hopeful substitute for precise utterance to strangers.

"Like" used to connect ideas. Now it replaces them.

"Right?" used to be a challenge. Now it is padding.

"I mean" must have meant something sometime.

Obviously, it is deplorable that these words have taken over the language. But this doesn't mean we should wait forever to recognize them. No, we must face facts and put them in our books:

"Friends, Romans, countrymen . . . lend me your ears . . . I mean . . . I come to bury Caesar . . . right? . . . not to . . . you know . . . praise him."

"By the shores of Gitchee . . . you know . . . Gumee,

"I mean . . . By the shining Big-Sea-Water . . . right?

"Stood the . . . like . . . wigwam of Nokomis,

"Daughter of the . . . you know . . . Moon, Nokomis."

"Like . . . fourscore and . . . you know . . . seven years ago . . . right? . . . our fathers . . . like . . . brought forth . . . I mean . . . on this continent a new . . . like . . . nation . . ."

Anyone, of course, is welcome to disagree. I mean, like, you know, right?

Ways to Write Better Letters

BY J. HAROLD JANIS

A neighbor of mine recently wrote two contractors for bids on a concrete driveway. Here's the beginning of one reply: "Dear Mr. ————: I am offering you a special price because I am having a slack season now. I have some debts to pay and this work will be a big help to me."

The second began: "Dear Mr. ————: I can give you a good, solid driveway with a six-inch bed of cinders and three inches of concrete. Properly graded and drained, this should last you 20 years without cracking."

The second man got the job. Why? Because he told my neighbor what he wanted to know, not how much good the job would do the contractor. He followed the first principle of good letter-writing, think of *your reader's* problems, not of your own.

The letters we write can spell the difference between making and missing an important sale, between landing and losing a job, between a yes or no from the girl of our dreams.

When applying for a job by letter, it is tempting for the writer to talk exclusively about himself, his aims, his desires. I have seen letters of application which began like this: "Dear Sir: I am just the man you described in your advertisement, and I am interested in a new job just now because I am not satisfied with my present position. . . ." This is a weak approach. A prospective employer is seldom as interested in an applicant's need for the job as he is in his own need for filling it.

The second rule for effective letter writing is: *Be yourself*. The best letters are written as we would talk. The windy artificial formulas are out of place. The businessman who uses such phrases as "Yours of the 14th in hand . . . ," "Agreeable to your communication of July 23 . . . ," gives the impression that he's a pompous old egotist with no friendly feeling for the person he's writing.

The next rule is: *Be thrifty with words*. Recently one of my students began a letter for his boss like this: "In reply to your letter calling attention to the fact that we sent you the wrong number of two-tone men's oxfords, we wish to apologize for our error." When I suggested that he cut out every unessential word, he came back with this result: "The error is ours and we're sorry." *That* letter said what it meant, clearly, and omitted all unnecessary information.

My Aunt Clara lives in a small town in Oklahoma, and it sounds like a wonderful place when she describes it. "It's so warm for April," she wrote me last spring, "that the trees are practically bursting into leaf, and old Mrs. Johnson is in the back-yard swing next door thawing out her Arthuritis, as she calls it."

Clara's sister, Emily, lives in the same neighborhood, and I got a letter from her last April, too. "You can't imagine how hot and dry and uncomfortable it is for early spring," she wrote. "This probably means another dreadful summer and a drought. Poor Mrs. Johnson is very uncomfortable from arthritis, and hardly ever moves any more."

It's easy to see why everyone prefers to hear from Clara. She follows another important rule: *Accent the positive*.

Even in writing a note of condolence it is possible to be positive and comforting. Such expressions as "Our hearts ache for you" are usually sincere, but hopeful, forward-looking ideas can make such letters even more comforting and helpful.

Here is a note of condolence a woman received from one of her husband's colleagues: "Dear Julie: Martha and I are thinking of you today, and we know that with God's help you are going ahead bravely. Down at the lab yesterday we were talking about the project that you know was closest to Bob's heart. Everyone is determined to carry it forward with more energy than ever. You see, his work will always be an inspiration, and we'll never feel that he's far from our side."

In business letters this upbeat accent is extremely important. A building-materials supplier found that his new type of shingle, although superior, was not selling as well as an older style had. It turned out that the man handling orders was writing the following letter to customers: "Dear Mr. ———: I am sorry to tell you we no longer handle the kind of shingle you inquired about. We have, however, a new style which may fit your needs."

This apologetic, negative approach was changed as follows: "Dear Mr. ———: I am happy to send you samples of our new shingle, which comes in a wider range of colors and textures than the shingle that you inquired about. It is a great improvement on the old style, which it has replaced."

Both letters told the truth, but the second took a positive approach. Sales began to rise immediately.

It is surprising how many letters disclose an unintentional antagonism. The other day my wife received this note from a store: "As you claim one of the cups you ordered arrived with a broken handle, we will have to replace it." The management presumably didn't doubt my wife's word, but a sneaking accusation of dishonesty is implied in "you claim." Why hadn't they just written: "We are sorry that one of the cups you ordered arrived broken. Of course, we will replace it immediately."

Some years ago I was asked to help improve the correspondence of a number of agencies of the City of New York. Many letters from city offices were intended to soothe irate citizens, yet had the opposite effect. I discovered a letter sent by one department which said: "If you will send us a sample of your product, we will determine its practical value, if any."

I lectured on the need for making letters express a courteous, helpful attitude. One man, after carrying on a long argument by mail with a particularly angry taxpayer tried the following: "Dear Mrs. Brown: Believe it or not, this office is here to help you with your problem."

In her next letter Mrs. Brown confessed that she had been more irritated by the tone of the letters she had been getting than by the problem she was trying to solve.

Beyond all the rules, however, there is an indefinable quality or tone in a letter which comes directly from the personality of the writer. It can't be taught, but it can be learned. This letter, written by William E. Robinson, when he was elected president of the Coca Cola Co., will show what I mean: "Dear ———: You are a generous and thoughtful friend to take the trouble to write me about my new job. I deeply appreciate your good wishes, to which I hope you may add a prayer or two. There are bound to be occasions when I will need both. My thanks—and only the best."

Notice the informality and the brevity. This letter says no more than is necessary, yet there is no feeling of haste or abruptness. Given thought and care, every letter we write can be similarly effective.

Word Power Test No. 4

People, Beasts and Places

BY PETER FUNK

The English poet William Cowper thought of word-lovers as huntsmen

> "... who chase
> A panting syllable through time and space,
> Start it at home, and hunt it in the dark,
> To Gaul, to Greece, and into Noah's ark."

In the test below, you need not range quite that far back into antiquity; yet each of these words, if chased to its origin, will prove to have sprung from the name or a characteristic of a person, animal or place—real or imaginary. Check the word or phrase you believe is *nearest in meaning* to the key word. Answers appear at the end of this test.

1. **tawdry** (taw′ drē)—A: dilatory. B: offensive. C: sandy-colored. **D**: gaudily cheap.
2. **amazon** (am′ ă zŏn)—A: mythological god. B: wild animal. **C**: tall, strong woman. D: skeptic.
3. **Pollyanna** (pŏl ē an′ ă)—one who is: A: old-fashioned. B: cranky. **C**: invincibly optimistic. D: extremely cautious.
4. **draconian** (drā kō′ nē an)—A: orderly. **B**: frightening. C: harsh. D: benign.
5. **Machiavellian** (măk ē ă věl′ ē an)—A: wicked. B: practical. C: straightforward. **D**: crafty.
6. **boycott** (boy′ kŏt)—A: to accuse of wrongdoing. B: withdraw from. **C**: refuse to deal with. D: keep silence.
7. **meandering** (mē an′ der ing)—A: complaining. B: murmuring. C: cascading. **D**: winding or turning.

8. **chauvinism** (shō′ vĭ nizm)—A: extreme partiality. B: conceit. C: fairmindedness. D: piety.

9. **forum** (for′ um)—A: recess. B: place of public discussion. C: dispersion. D: small chamber.

10. **babel** (bā′ b'l)—A: weight-lifting device. B: confusion of voices. C: clear message. D: small gem.

11. **hackneyed** (hăk′ nēd)—A: fragmented. B: trite. C: unfashionable. D: compelling.

12. **protean** (prō′ tē an)—A: nutritious. B: fascinating. C: changeable. D: deceitful.

13. **spartan** (spar′ t'n)—A: austere. B: hardheaded. C: energetic. D: forbidding.

14. **panacea** (pan ă sē′ ă)—A: uproar. B: praise. C: cure-all. D: overall view.

15. **crestfallen** (krest′ faw len)—A: jubilant. B: impecunious. C: dejected. D: fearful.

16. **philander** (fĭ lan′ der)—to be a: A: spendthrift. B: frivolous lover. C: donor. D: procrastinator.

17. **utopia** (ū tō′ pē a)—A: an ideal place. B: practical concept. C: desired goal. D: lesion.

18. **robot** (rō′ bŏt)—A: automatic device. B: skiff. C: any machine. D: skilled technician.

19. **shanghai** (shang′ hī)—A: to estimate. B: plunder. C: abduct. D: free.

20. **marathon** (măr′ ă thon)—A: tedious repetition. B: long-distance race. C: Greek temple. D: seasonal wind.

ANSWERS

1. **tawdry**—D: Anything *tawdry* is cheap and gaudy. Lace neckpieces, named after *St. Audrey,* were sold at an annual medieval fair. In time, the quality of lace became inferior and the saint's name was shortened.

2. **amazon**—C: Any tall, strong woman. In Greek mythology the *Amazons* were a race of female warriors.

3. **Pollyanna**—C: One who is invincibly optimistic. After *Pollyanna*, young heroine of a novel by Eleanor H. Porter (1868–1920).

4. **draconian**—C: Harsh; rigorous; severe; as, *draconian* punishment. After *Draco*, a strict Greek lawgiver in the 7th century B.C., who prescribed death for almost every offense.

5. **Machiavellian**—D: Crafty; deceitful; politically unscrupulous; as, *Machiavellian* schemes. From Niccolo *Machiavelli*, 16th-century Italian diplomat.

6. **boycott**—C: To unite in refusing to have anything to do with the products or services of a person or group. From Capt. Charles *Boycott*, an Irish land agent ostracized by tenants when he raised rents.

7. **meandering**—D: Winding or turning; as, a *meandering* stream. From *Maiandros*, an ancient Greek river famous for its winding course.

8. **chauvinism**—A: Extreme partiality; blind patriotism. From Nicolas *Chauvin*, a soldier who worshiped Napoleon as a hero without fault.

9. **forum**—B: Place of gathering for public discussion. After the marketplace in Roman cities that were used for judicial and public business.

10. **babel**—B: Confusion of voices, sounds, languages. From the city and tower of *Babel* in the Bible (Gen. 11:4–9).

11. **hackneyed**—B: Trite; stale; as, a *hackneyed* slogan. Named for the workaday riding horses from Hackney, a London borough.

12. **protean**—C: Changeable; assuming different forms; as, a *protean* actor. From *Proteus*, Greek sea god who was always changing form.

13. **spartan**—A: Austere; as, a *spartan* existence. From the extreme plainness of *Sparta*, a Greek city-state.

14. **panacea**—C: Cure-all; remedy for all ills and difficulties. Asclepius, the Greek god of medicine, named one of his daughters *Panakeia* (the all-healing); hence our word today.

15. **crestfallen**—C: Dejected; dispirited; downcast. From a rooster's crest, which literally droops when he loses a fight.

16. **philander**—B: To make love frivolously. *Philander* was the name given to lovers in medieval romances and came from the Greek *philandros* (one who loves).

17. **utopia**—A: An imaginary, ideal place where all things are perfect. From *Utopia*, a fictional country in the book of that name by Sir Thomas More (1516). Greek *ou* (no) and *topos* (place).

18. **robot**—A: Automatic device that operates with human skill; a person who works mechanically. From the Czech *robotnik* (slave), from *robota* (forced labor).

19. **shanghai**—C: Abduct; compel by force, fraud or trickery. From the practice of procuring sailors for long voyages, perhaps originally to *Shanghai*, by kidnapping.

20. **marathon**—B: Long-distance race. In 490 B.C. 10,000 Athenians defeated 100,000 Persians at the battle of *Marathon*. A Greek—running the first *"marathon"*—brought the news to the city of Athens 26 miles away.

VOCABULARY RATINGS

20—18 correct ....exceptional
17—15 correct ....excellent
14—12 correct ....good

Classroom Classics

Schoolboy Howlers Which Make Examination Papers Lively Reading

EDITED BY ALEXANDER ABINGDON

Definitions

Acrimony, sometimes called holy, is another name for marriage.

Cubism is the rules of very young Scouts.

Filet Mignon is an opera by Puccini.

A hamlet is a little pig.

Hygiene is keeping clean when it is not essential.

A polygon is a man with more than one wife, preferably living.

Teetotalers are boys who carry golf clubs. They are generally paid, except in Scotland.

Sinister means a woman who hasn't married.

Politics

The President has the power to appoint and disappoint the members of his Cabinet.

A Conservative is a kind of greenhouse where you look at the moon.

Geography

The climate of Bombay is such that its inhabitants have to live elsewhere.

The equator is a menagerie lion running around the earth and through Africa.

Denver is just below the "o" in Colorado.

They don't raise anything in Kansas but Alpaca Grass, and they have to irritate that to make it grow.

History

Cleopatra ended a remarkable life rather curiously. She was bitten by an aspidistra.

In preparation for the channel crossing, Caesar built 18 new vesuls vessils vesles botes.

1066 is in the ninth century because centuries always for some reason or other fall back one.

Henry VIII had an abbess on his knee, which made walking difficult.

The father of the famous Black Prince in English history was Old King Cole.

Queen Elizabeth was the "Virgin Queen." As a queen she was a success.

Hygiene

For fainting: rub the person's chest, or if a lady, rub her arm above the hand.

There are four symptoms of a cold. Two I forget and the other two are too well known to mention.

Doctors today say that fatal diseases are the worst.

False doctrine means giving people the wrong medicine.

Miscellaneous

The greatest miracle in the Bible is when Joshua told his son to stand still and he obeyed him.

After sinking a shaft 100 feet at the mine, they finally struck bedpan.

Are We Becoming a Nation of Illiterates?

BY VANCE PACKARD

A young man who calls himself Peter Doe gave the U.S. educational system a bad case of the shakes. In 1974 he sued the San Francisco Unified School District for half a million dollars because it awarded him a high-school diploma even though he was barely literate.

Tests both before and after graduation allegedly indicated that he was reading at the fifth- or sixth-grade level when he received his diploma. He contends that, in the outside world of work, he quickly found himself handicapped by deficiency in writing skills. He wanted to work as a clothing salesman but, in applying for jobs, he found that he could not cope with application forms.

Peter is a white, middle-class student who attended his classes regularly and was not considered a disciplinary problem. What worries educators is that there are probably tens of thousands of other high-school graduates like him. At a conference of educators, lawyers and judges in Washington, D.C., one judge warned that the case could bring down a host of suits which might cost billions of dollars. That seems plausible, for federal studies have discovered that seven million school youngsters have *severe* reading problems.

SHOCKING SHORTCOMINGS. Peter Doe's case illustrates a broad, worrisome trend: the general low state of literacy and ability to write clearly among younger and older people alike. And this at a time when the complexity of our institutions calls for ever-higher literacy just to function effectively. We must cope with insurance and employment forms, applications for medical coverage, applications for credit, auto-licensing forms—and so on and on. If we can't, we are what are known as "functional illiterates."

A survey by the Louis Harris organization found in 1971 that close to 19 million Americans over the age of 16 had difficulty coping with minimal measures of literacy such as application forms. The Pacific Telephone and Telegraph Company annually interviews tens of thousands of high-school graduates for jobs. Forty percent who apply fail because they can't read or write at the eighth-grade level.

For late-teenage students as a whole, the most dramatic evidence of decline in literacy emerges from the Scholastic Aptitude Test (SAT). Each year more than a million high-school seniors and juniors have been taking the SAT verbal test, and their scores correlate quite consistently with both their reading and their writing ability. *For ten straight years, the average score has been dropping*. Over the past decade it has dropped 35 points, or about seven percent.

Perhaps the most unflattering picture of the "reading comprehension" of young Americans, however, emerged from a survey conducted by the International Association for the Evaluation of Educational Achievement in 1970. When American youngsters are compared with the youth of nine European countries on a standard-score basis, American 14-year-olds are in the top four, but our 10-year-olds show up next to last.

Writing with easy clarity is crucial to our capacity to formulate our thoughts or communicate on the job. Yet ineptness at writing is found at all educational levels. The most extensive study of writing ability ever undertaken is under way in Denver at the federally funded National Assessment of Educational Progress. Its first national sampling of nearly 100,000 Americans was an eye-opener. By age 13 only the best of the students could cope with the basic conventions of writing. (This was after eight years of schooling!) By age 17 about half the students could put together simple sentences and express simple ideas in general, imprecise language; but three quarters of them misspelled at least one word, and more than half made errors in choice of words.

Young adults, however, provided the biggest surprise. When asked to write a letter to a public official opposing or supporting the building of a highway interchange in their community, 29 percent balked at even attempting the exercise.

WHY THE DECLINE? To explain the evident sag in both writing and reading, I would advance seven principal explanations.

1. Writing as an educational subject has lost status. English composition was once taught from third grade through college. Now it, like reading, is usually not taught much beyond sixth grade, except as an option or as a remedial course.

There is a common assumption in schools that students will somehow absorb writing skills while doing their work in other courses. Thus, after grade six there is little testing for literacy skills and, in most schools, papers are rarely corrected for anything except the most glaring errors in usage or spelling.

2. The growing use of multiple-choice questions for testing reading, writing and other subjects. Multiple-choice questions can be answered by making check marks, which permits fast visual grading, and by punching holes in a test sheet, which permits machine grading. But, by making checks or punching holes, the student does not have to choose his own words or organize his thoughts.

3. The overloading of English teachers and instructors with students. Tens of thousands of these mentors just don't have time to give much individual attention to students unless they work 70-hour weeks. They are typically held responsible for teaching at least 150 students. Correcting papers in a thoughtful, careful way takes a lot of time. Under pressure, many teachers simply scribble a couple of words of comment at the end of a theme.

4. The widespread sale of term papers on college campuses. With the growing impersonality of large colleges, firms selling term papers have been proliferating. A student can buy a ten-page paper for $29. But in the process he deprives himself of the important practice of formulating his own thoughts and putting them on paper.

5. *Automatic promotion in schools, open admissions to colleges.* The fact of compulsory education has led many school administrators in recent years to tolerate virtually automatic grade promotions. This has lessened the pressures on teachers to bear down on literacy skills. And the egalitarian concept that every youth who can drift up through high school or its equivalent is entitled to have a try at college has caused some big state institutions to throw open their gates. Result: a multitude of students enter who are reading at an eighth-grade level or lower.

6. *A revolt against rules and established ways.* As the "hang-loose" ethic took hold among millions of young people starting in the late 1960s, anything suggesting the value of disciplined practice or respect for the "mechanics" of writing was widely scorned. There was a shift to stress on spontaneity, creativity and "feelings," with less concern about conciseness or lucidity in writing. By 1972 the Council for Basic Education concluded that permissiveness "holds sway in the teaching of English today."

7. *Finally, and perhaps most important, the unanticipated side effects of the telecommunications revolution.* Voice cassettes, television, video-tape machines and telephones in every room have been applauded as marvelous techniques for simplifying communication. Even books now are being marketed in abbreviated form on voice cassettes. For millions, these devices are reducing much of the need for frequent practice in reading and writing. Writing is less in demand; some say it lacks "contemporary relevance."

Polls have shown that most Americans now get most of their news about the outside world from TV news programs. That is hardly as efficient as scanning hundreds of items in a newspaper in far less time. Av Westin, executive producer of ABC evening news, frankly concedes the shortcomings inherent in TV news. He says: "*I* know what we have to leave out; if people do not read newspapers, news magazines and books they are desperately uninformed."

TURNAROUND? Fortunately, enough people are becoming concerned about the low state of literacy in America so that something is being done about it. The federal Office of Education has launched a multi-million-dollar "Right to Read" program in 31 states. The aim is to improve reading skills in areas where they are not otherwise likely to develop. Classes are being set up for adolescent dropouts and in schools where a large number of students have serious reading problems. The Peter Doe lawsuit has inspired San Francisco to re-examine its reading requirements for high-school graduation. New York City is abandoning its practice of giving automatic promotion to virtually all students, and no student will receive a diploma if he is more than a year behind in reading.

Methods of teaching reading are changing. The predominant way reading has been taught for many years in U.S. schools is the "whole word" method. The reading texts build on such whole words as "Dick and Jane go to the store." According to critics such as the Council for Basic Education, many first-grade readers in use today have only about 350 words—yet the average first-grader has a listening vocabulary of about 15,000 words. The critics feel the pupil can more swiftly learn to read most of those 15,000 words by the phonics approach. Under this method, used by the television programs "Sesame Street" and "The Electric Company," they learn visually to recognize key elements used to build almost all words. For example, at, cat, hat; or eat, meat, heat. About one American child in five now in school is using phonics, and the number increases each year.

There are today some widely accepted approaches for improving writing skills, too. From third grade through college, for example, study programs are being arranged to assure that every student writes at least one page every day. As far as possible, students have a choice of subject matter, and their writing is checked for clarity and spelling as well as context.

Finally, two major assessment programs agree that the home where interesting reading materials are readily available plays a major role in a child's achieving a high state of literacy. The home, therefore, is the place where we should begin our crusade.

Word Power Test No. 5

English from Greece, Rome and Elsewhere

BY PETER FUNK

Scan this list of words and you will get a quick tour of some of the lands from which our words come: ancient Greece and Rome, France, Italy and Old England. Check the word or phrase you believe is nearest in meaning to the key word. Answers appear at the end of this test.

1. **amnesty** (am′ nes tē)—A: pardon. B: international agreement. C: ceasefire. D: diplomatic immunity.
2. **futile** (fū′ til)—A: easy. B: useless. C: productive. D: frustrating.
3. **elaborate** (e lab′ o rāt)—A: to be fussy. B: decorate. C: be elegant. D: develop.
4. **deterrent** (de tĕr′ ent)—A: cleansing substance. B: defense. C: restraint of action. D: warning.
5. **caldron** (kol′ dron)—A: tomb. B: barrier. C: whirlpool. D: kettle.
6. **resuscitate** (re sus′ ĭ tāt)—A: to withdraw. B: revive. C: quiet. D: exhume.
7. **callow** (kăl′ ō)—A: tough. B: lacking depth. C: inexperienced. D: sickly yellow.
8. **trivia** (triv′ ĭ a)—A: trifles. B: chatter. C: harmful material. D: travel notes.
9. **purport** (pur′ port)—A: concept. B: forecast. C: scope. D: meaning.
10. **cadaverous** (ka dăv′ er us)—A: empty. B: gaunt. C: frightening. D: huge.
11. **denigrate** (den′ ĭ grāt)—A: to demean oneself. B: disavow. C: assign. D: defame.
12. **virtuoso** (vir tū ō′ sō)—A: dilettante. B: good person. C: expert. D: violinist.

13. **tendentious** (ten den′ shus)—A: pompous. B: biased. C: long-winded. D: belligerent.

14. **cumulative** (kū′ mū la tiv; -lāt iv)—A: steadily increasing. B: cloud-like. C: fully developed. D: collected.

15. **decorous** (dek′ o rus)—A: beautiful. B: proper. C: artistic. D: modest.

16. **ebullient** (e bul′ yent)—A: enthusiastic. B: stubborn. C: forceful. D: swollen.

17. **vandalism** (van′ dal iz m)—A: banditry. B: vagrancy. C: destruction. D: beggary.

18. **leonine** (lē′ o nīn)—A: wild. B: haughty. C: flowing. D: lion-like.

19. **abridge** (a brij′)—A: to condense. B: arch or bend. C: join. D: cross.

20. **skeptic** (skep′ tik)—A: dissenter. B: bigot. C: doubter. D: heckler.

ANSWERS

1. **amnesty**—A: General pardon, as by a government, for past offenses; as, to grant *amnesty* to all political exiles. Greek *amnēstia* (forgetfulness).

2. **futile**—B: Useless; fruitless; of no avail; as, a *futile* effort, Latin *futilis*.

3. **elaborate**—D: To develop thoroughly; work out in detail; as, to *elaborate* a housing plan. Latin *elaborare* (to work out).

4. **deterrent**—C: Prevention or restraint of action, as by fear of consequences; as, a nuclear *deterrent* to aggression. Latin *deterrere* (to frighten from).

5. **caldron**—D: Large kettle or pot; as, a boiling *caldron* of unrest. Latin *calere* (to be warm).

6. **resuscitate**—B: To revive, especially from unconsciousness; as, to *resuscitate* a victim of electrical shock. Latin *resuscitare* (to rouse again).

7. **callow**—C: Inexperienced; unsophisticated; immature; (originally, of a bird: unfledged; lacking feathers to fly); as, a *callow* student. Old English *calu* (bald).

8. **trivia**—A: Trifles; unimportant matters; as, a mind cluttered with *trivia*. Latin *trivium* (crossroads).

9. **purport**—D: Conveyed or implied meaning; import; also,

substance; gist; as, the *purport* of a speech. Old French *porporter* (to convey).

10. **cadaverous**—B: Gaunt; emaciated; corpselike; as, a *cadaverous* patient. Latin *cadaver* (dead body)..

11. **denigrate**—D: To defame; cast aspersions on; malign; as, to *denigrate* a public official. Latin *denigrare* (to blacken).

12. **virtuoso**—C: Expert; one having masterly skill or brilliance; as, a renowned piano *virtuoso*. Italian *virtuoso* (skilled).

13. **tendentious**—B: Biased; partial; tending to favor a particular point of view; as, a *tendentious* reporter. Latin *tendere* (to be inclined, tend).

14. **cumulative**—A: Steadily increasing; growing by successive additions; as, *cumulative* knowledge. Latin *cumulare* (to heap up).

15. **decorous**—B: Proper; exhibiting good taste; correct; as, *decorous* behavior. Latin *decor* (beauty, grace).

16. **ebullient**—A: Enthusiastic; lively; exuberant; as, an *ebullient* host. Latin *ebullire* (to bubble out).

17. **vandalism**—C: Malicious destruction or defacement of public or private property; as, an outbreak of *vandalism* in the schools. From *Vandal,* one of an ancient Germanic tribe which in the fifth century sacked Rome.

18. **leonine**—D: Resembling or suggesting a lion; as, a *leonine* head. Latin *leo* (lion).

19. **abridge**—A: To condense; shorten by omitting words without changing or losing sense; as, to *abridge* a long novel. Latin *abbreviare* (to shorten).

20. **skeptic**—C: Doubter; one who questions generally accepted beliefs, doctrines or theories; as, a religious *skeptic*. Greek *skeptikos* (reflective, thoughtful).

VOCABULARY RATINGS

20—18 correct ....exceptional
17—15 correct ....excellent
14—12 correct .... good

Write the Way
You Talk

BY RUDOLF FLESCH

Ninety-nine percent of the people who come to my writing classes were born non-writers and have stayed that way all their lives. For them, writing has always been an unpleasant chore; answering a simple letter looms ahead like a visit to the dentist. But they have to do a certain amount of writing in their careers. And knowing their writing was poor, they decided to do something about it.

No doubt when you think about improving your writing, you think of grammar, rhetoric, composition,—all those dull things you learned year after year in school. But most likely, these things are not your problem. You probably have a pretty good grip on these essentials. What you need is instruction in the basic principles of professional writing.

Why professional writing? Because you now write as you did in school, unconsciously trying to please the teacher by following the rules of "English composition." You're not really writing a letter to the addressee, or a report for your vice president. The pros—magazine writers, newspapermen, novelists, people who write for a living—learned long ago that they must use "spoken" English and avoid "written" English like the plague.

TALK ON PAPER. The secret to more effective writing is simple: *talk* to your reader. Pretend the person who'll read your letter or report is sitting across from you, or that you are on the phone with him. Be informal. Relax. Talk in your ordinary voice, your ordinary manner, vocabulary, accent and expression. You wouldn't say "Please be advised," or "We wish to inform you." Instead, something like, "You see, it's like this," or "Let me explain this." One helpful trick is to imagine yourself talking to your reader across a table at lunch. Punctuate your sentences in your mind, with a bite from a sandwich. Intersperse your thoughts with an occasional "you know," or the person's name.

So talk—talk on paper. Go over what you've written. Does it look and sound like talk? If not, change it until it does.

USE CONTRACTIONS FREELY. There's nothing more important for improving your writing style. Use of *don't* and *it's* and *haven't* and *there's* is the No. 1 style device of modern professional writing. Once you've learned this basic trick, you can start producing prose that will be clear, informal and effective.

Take the standard opening phrase: "Enclosed please find." What's a better way of saying that? Simply, "Here's"!*

LEAVE OUT THE WORD "THAT" WHENEVER POSSIBLE. You can often omit it without changing the meaning at all. Take this sentence: "We suggest that you send us your passbook once a year." Now strike out *that*. Isn't this better and smoother? Again, this is something we do all the time in speaking.

And while you're crossing out *thats*, also go on a *which* hunt. For some reason people think *which* is a more elegant pronoun. Wrong. Usually you can replace *which* by *that*, or leave it out altogether—and you'll get a better, more

---

*Though most of my examples are taken from business correspondence, the principles apply to *all* types of writing.

fluent, more "spoken" sentence.

USE DIRECT QUESTIONS. A conversation is not one-sided. One person speaks, then the other interrupts, often with a question, like "Really?" or "Then what?" A conversation without questions is almost inconceivable. So use a question whenever there's an opportunity, and your writing will sound more like talk.

You don't have to go out of your way to do this. Look at what you write and you'll find indirect questions—beginning with *whether* all over the place. "Please determine whether payment against these receipts will be in order." No good. Make it: "Can we pay against these receipts? Please find out and let us know."

Or take another sentence: "Your questions and comments are invited." Again, this is really a question: "Do you have any questions or comments? If so, please let us know." There's nothing like a direct question to get some feedback.

USE PERSONAL PRONOUNS. A speaker uses *I, we* and *you* incessantly—they're part of the give-and-take of conversation. Everybody, it seems, who writes for a company or organization clings desperately to the passive voice and avoids taking the slightest responsibility. He doesn't say *we*, never says *I*, and he even avoids using the straightforward *you*. So we find phrases like "It is assumed . . ." "it will be seen . . ." "it is recommended. . . ." Or sentences like: "An investigation is being made and upon its completion a report will be furnished you." Instead, write, "We've made an investigation and we'll furnish you a report."

Normally, when writing for an organization, there isn't too much opportunity to say "I." But do use "I" whenever you express feelings and thoughts that are your own. Often it's better to say "I'm sorry" or "we're pleased," than "we're sorry" or "we're pleased." And call the addressee *you*. The idea is to make your writing as personal as possible.

IT'S ALL RIGHT TO PUT PREPOSITIONS AT THE END. For 50 years, English-language experts have unanimously insisted that a preposition at the end is fine and dandy. H. W. Fowler, in *A Dictionary of Modern English Usage,* 1926, defends it enthusiastically and cites examples from Shakespeare and the Bible to Thackeray and

Kipling. Yet schoolteachers still tell pupils they should never commit such a wicked crime.

Put the preposition at the end whenever it sounds right to do so. Instead of "The claimant is not entitled to the benefits for which he applied," write "The claimant isn't entitled to the benefits he applied for." Remember, grammatical superstitions are something to get rid of.

SPILL THE BEANS. There's a natural tendency in all of us to begin at the beginning and go on to the end. When you write a letter, it's the easiest way to organize your material. The trouble is, it's hard on the reader. He has a problem, or a question, and wants to know whether the answer is yes or no. If he has to wait until you're willing to tell him, his impatience and subconscious resentment will increase with every word. Rather than stumbling your way through some awkward introduction, start right in with the most important thing you want to get across. Plunge right in.

Re: . . .

Gentlemen:

In reference to the above collection item, which you instructed us to hold at the disposal of the beneficiary, we wish to advise that Mr. Ling has not called on us, nor have we received any inquiries on his behalf.

The above information is provided to you in the event you wish to give us any further instructions in the matter.

Cross out everything up to the words "Mr. Ling." Then the letter becomes (with a few other minor changes):

Re: . . .

Gentlemen:

Mr. Ling hasn't called on us, nor have we had any inquiries on his behalf. Do you have any further instructions?

You see what this does? Once the unnecessary verbiage is cleared away, the letter becomes downright elegant.

WRITE SHORT, SNAPPY SENTENCES. The ordinary reader can take in only so many words before his eyes come to a brief rest at a period. If a sentence has more than 40 words, chances are he's been unable to take in the full meaning. So break those long sentences apart, 20 words at most. It's usually quite easy to see where one idea leaves off and another begins. Then try writing *really* short sentences every so often, and watch your letters and reports wake from their customary torpor.

USE SHORT WORDS. Long, pompous words are a curse, a curtain that comes between writer and reader. Here are some familiar sayings as they would appear in a business letter. "In the event that initially you fail to succeed, endeavor, endeavor again." "All is well that terminates well."

Everybody has his own pet pomposities. Banish them from your vocabulary. Replace *locate* with *find; prior to* with *before; sufficient* with *enough; in the event that* with *if.* After those simple substitutions, weed out such other words as *determine, facilitate* and *require* whenever they show up. You'll find that it's possible to live without them. And you'll learn to appreciate the joys of simple language.

WRITE FOR PEOPLE. By far the most important thing is to give your letters just the right human touch. Express your natural feelings. If it's good news, say you're glad; if it's bad news, say you're sorry. Be as courteous, polite and interested as you'd be if the addressee sat in front of you. Some human being will read your letter and, consciously or unconsciously, be annoyed if it is cold, pleased if you're courteous and friendly.

A bank got a letter from a customer who'd moved from New York to Bermuda. He wrote to make new arrangements about his account. The bank's answer started: "We thank you for your letter advising us of your change of address." Now really! How stony and unfeeling can you get? I would at least have said something like "I noted your new address with envy."

You'll find there are rewards for improving your written work. This is the age of large organizations where it's easier to catch the eye of a superior by what you write than by what you say or do. Write the way I suggest and your stuff will stand out. Beyond the material rewards are more personal ones. When you write a particularly crisp, elegant paragraph, or a letter that conveys your thoughts clearly and simply, you'll feel a flow of creative achievement. Treasure it. It's something you've earned.

A Civil Tongue

High crimes and misdemeanors are being visited on American English, mourns this observer, and few of us can escape impeachment

BY EDWIN NEWMAN

A civil tongue means to me a language that is not bogged down in jargon, not puffed up with false dignity, not studded with trick phrases that have lost their meaning.

It is not falsely exciting, is not patronizing, does not conceal the smallness and triteness of ideas by clothing them in language ever more grandiose, does not seek out increasingly complicated constructions.

It treats errors in spelling and usage with a decent tolerance but does not take them lightly. It is direct, specific, concrete, vigorous, colorful, subtle and imaginative when it should be, and as lucid and eloquent as we are able to make it. It is something to revel in and enjoy.

Unfortunately, it is also only a dream, for an ironic thing is happening in the United States. As we demand more and more personal openness from those in public life, our language becomes more and more covered, obscure, turgid, ponderous and overblown.

Nelson Rockefeller, for example, when asked whether he would be nominated at the 1976 Republican convention, said, "I cannot conceive of any scenario in which that could eventuate."

Won't things improve when the younger generation of politicians takes over? No.

California's Gov. Edmund Brown, Jr., 39, asked whether his 1976 Presidential candidacy was really aimed at 1980, replied, "My equation is sufficiently complex to admit of various outcomes." Declining to ride to a money-raising dinner in a chauffeur-driven Mercedes, he explained, "I cannot relate to that material possessory consciousness," and used an unwashed Ford instead.

Stuffiness and fake erudition are being substituted for reality and clarity. Instead of teachers encouraging our schoolchildren, according to a study in the *Journal of Educational Psychology,* teachers are "reinforcing" the children by a process of "emission." The educational advantage in saying emitting reinforcers rather than encouraging children—or, for that matter, calling a teacher a facilitator or enabler, a teaching period a module, and a classroom a learning station—escapes me.

Fortunately, practitioners of a civil tongue do exist. A reporter asked AFL-CIO head George Meany about the election of November 1974. What was the people's mandate? Said Meany: "I don't believe in this mandate stuff. A guy runs for office and gets elected. All of a sudden he's got a mandate. Two less votes and he's nothing."

A civil tongue knows when to remain silent. In September 1974, Prime Minister Pierre Trudeau of Canada decided not to come to the United Nations and speak because he had nothing sufficiently important to say. At the Democratic convention in 1976, a reporter asked eight-year-old Amy Carter whether she had a message for the children of America. Said Amy: "No." Such gestures deserve more notice.

I once went to Sauk Centre, Minn., for a television story about a festival honoring Sinclair Lewis, who was born there. A local resident said of a task that was facing us, "It's more than the horse can pull." We city boys thought that amusingly bucolic, but in seven words it's hard to say more.

Usually our use of words is extravagant. The waste has two causes. One is the feeling that an idea is more effective if it is repeated and reinforced. This is why Jimmy Carter says that he had a "deeply profound" religious experience. (At any rate, I want to believe that that is why. I would hate to learn that he thought that deep and profound are different.) In 1975, Sen. Charles Percy of Illinois warned fellow Republicans against choosing a Presidential nominee not in the "centrist mainstream" of U.S. politics. Dr. John Lungren, looking after Richard Nixon, said in January 1975, "He still tires and fatigues very easily."

The second cause of waste in our use of words is an apparent failure to understand what they mean. If it knew what surprise meant, the *New York Times* could not run a headline about an "unexpected surprise" from Japan. Lt. Gen. James F. Hollingsworth, former U.S. commander in South Korea, said that if the North Koreans attack, "our firepower will have a tremendous impact on their ground troops, breaking their will to fight in addition to killing them."

The sports and business worlds make their contributions to the nonsense around us. Broadcasters tell us about the baseball team "with the worst record won and lostwise," about the football player who incurs a penalty and becomes the "guilty culprit." An airline stewardess urges her passengers to "have a nice day in Cincinnati or wherever your final destination may be taking you." And an investment company writes: "We have exceptional game plan capabilities together with strict concerns for programming successful situations."

American English, drawing on so many regional differences, so many immigrant groups, and such a range of business, farming, industrial, athletic and artistic experiences, can have an incomparable richness. Instead, high crimes and misdemeanors are visited upon it, and those who commit them do not understand that they are crimes against themselves. The language belongs to all of us. We have no more valuable possession.

Foreigners often have a peculiar talent for using English in an original way. After an earthquake in Italy, a local resident described the scene. "Dogs were complaining," he said, "and animals were shouting." I am trying not to shout, but I am complaining. Civilly. Most of the time.

Word Power Test No. 6

Words From *Reader's Digest*

BY PETER FUNK

The following test words have been taken from articles in *Reader's Digest*. Check the word or phrase you believe is *nearest in meaning* to the key word. Answers appear at the end of this test.

1. **parochial** (pa rō′ kǐ al)—A: religious. *B*: limited. C: pertaining to teaching. D: controversial.

2. **euphoria** (ū fō′ rǐ a)—*A*: sense of well-being. B: vagueness. C: enthusiasm. D: loss of memory.

3. **implicit** (im plis′ it)—A: accurate. B: obvious. *C*: understood. D: subtle.

4. **remorse** (rǐ mors′)—*A*: self-reproach. B: vengeance. C: pity. D: pride.

5. **aura** (aw′ ra)—A: crown. *B*: atmosphere. C: setting. D: piety.

6. **curfew** (kur′ few)—A: vespers. B: warning. *C*: restrictive regulation. D: bell tower.

7. **provocative** (pro vŏk′ a tiv)—A: noisy. B: pleading. C: cranky. *D*: stimulating.

8. **dexterity** (deks ter′ ǐ tē)—A: adroitness. *B*: precision. C: superficiality. D: vigor.

9. **ephemeral** (ĕ fem′ er al)—A: luminous. *B*: fragile. C: short-lived. D: oblivious.

10. **vituperative** (vī tū′ per a tiv; -ā tiv)—A: abusive. B: ugly. C: explosive. *D*: touchy.

11. **enigma** (ĕ nig′ ma)—A: nonsense. B: complication. *C*: puzzle. D: blemish.

12. **petrify** (pet′ rǐ fī)—A: to worry. B: bewilder. C: preserve. *D*: harden.

13. **quadrant** (kwod′ rant)—~~A~~: fourth of a circle. B: square dance. C: courtyard. D: singing group.

14. **collegial** (kŏ lē′ jĭ al)—relating to A: ancestral descent. B: assembly of diverse fragments. C: security for debt. ~~D~~: group of colleagues.

15. **indigent** (in′ dĭ jent)—A: native. B: poor. ~~C~~: angry. D: sick.

16. **matrix** (mā′ triks)—A: representative. ~~B~~: mold. C: older woman. D: church vestibule.

17. **propitious** (pro pish′ us)—A: ridiculous. B: favorable. ~~C~~: pushy. D: foreshadowed.

18. **infringe** (in frinj′)—A: to encircle. B: decorate. C: add to. ~~D~~: encroach.

19. **gregarious** (gre gair′ ē us)—A: sociable. B: talkative. C: casual. ~~D~~: jovial.

20. **contingent** (kon tin′ jent)—A: adjoining. B: dependent. ~~C~~: agreed upon. D: strict.

ANSWERS

1. **parochial**—B: Confined or restricted to a parish, hence limited in scope or outlook; narrow; as, a *parochial* viewpoint. Latin *parochia* (parish).

2. **euphoria**—A: Sense of well-being or elation, often unaccounted for; as, to experience frequent spells of *euphoria*. Greek *euphoros* (healthy).

3. **implicit**—C: Understood, though not expressed; implied; as, an *implicit* agreement; also, absolute; unquestioning; as, *implicit* faith. Latin *implicare* (to involve).

4. **remorse**—A: Self-reproach; intense anguish caused by guilt. Latin *remordere*, from *re* (again) and *mordere* (to bite). Your conscience "bites back" at you.

5. **aura**—B: Characteristic atmosphere or aspect; subtle radiance or air about a person or thing; as, an *aura* of success. Greek *aura* (air).

6. **curfew**—C: Regulation ordering persons off the streets and closing business establishments at a specified hour. Middle French *covrefeu* (to cover the fire)—a nightly signal during the Middle Ages to bank the hearth fire.

7. **provocative**—D: Stimulating; tending to excite, stir up or move profoundly; as, a *provocative* play. Latin *provocare* (to call forth).

8. **dexterity**—A: Adroitness; skill and ease in using the hands; mental skill or quickness. Latin *dexter* (skillful).

9. **ephemeral**—C: Short-lived; fleeting; transitory; as, *ephemeral* popularity. Greek *ephēmeros* (lasting a day).

10. **vituperative**—A: Abusive; scolding; railing; as, a *vituperative* rabble-rouser. Latin *vituperare* (to blame, abuse in words).

11. **enigma**—C: Puzzle; riddle; baffling problem; inscrutable or mysterious person. Greek *ainigma*, from *ainissesthai* (to speak in riddles).

12. **petrify**—D: To harden; convert into stone or stony substance; also, to confound or paralyze; as, to *petrify* with fear. Middle French *petrifier* (to turn to stone).

13. **quadrant**—A: One fourth of a circle; any of the four parts into which a plane is divided by two lines that intersect each other at right angles. Latin *quadrans* (fourth part).

14. **collegial**—D: Relating to a collegium or group of colleagues, each of whom has equal power and authority; as, a *collegial* board of trustees. Latin *collega* (colleague).

15. **indigent**—B: Poor; needy; as, *indigent* Eskimo children. Latin *indigere* (to want, need, stand in need of).

16. **matrix**—B: Mold within which anything develops or is contained. Late Latin *matrix* (womb).

17. **propitious**—B: Favorable; advantageous; opportune; as, a *propitious* moment. Latin *propitius*.

18. **infringe**—D: To encroach or trespass upon a right, prerogative or territory of another; violate; as, to *infringe* a treaty, patent or copyright. Latin *infringere* (to break off).

19. **gregarious**—A: Sociable; tending to associate with others; as, man's *gregarious* impulses. Latin *gregarius* (belonging to a herd or flock).

20. **contingent**—B: Dependent for effect on or liable to modification by something that may or may not occur; as, a *contingent* legacy. Latin *contingere* (to happen).

VOCABULARY RATINGS

20—18 correct ....exceptional
17—15 correct ....excellent
14—12 correct ....good

Was
Paul Revere a
Minute-person?

BY JACQUES BARZUN

Last spring, I received a committee report signed with two names. Each was identified as *Co-chairperson*. This designation was not new to me, but the pathos of attaching such a label to live fellow workers struck me with fresh force.

Obviously, the reason for using *person* was to avoid *man*, now felt to be the sign of an arrogant imperialism. In the background, no doubt, was the further wish to confirm equality by insisting on our common humanness. With that last intention no one will quarrel. But *man*, in *chairman* and elsewhere, still means and, etymologically, always has meant *person*. As far back as the Sanskrit *manus*, the root *man* means *human being*, with no implication of sex. The German *Mann* and *Mensch*, the Latin *homo* (from which derives the word *human*—and the *humanness* that we so passionately seek) originally denote the *kind* of creature we all are. *Homo sapiens* means male and female alike. Unless limited by context, *mankind* means and has always meant humanity entire.

The present urge to tamper with familiar usage is fool-ishly misdirected. Recently, a colleague gave a new sec-retary a note to type. He found it perfect, except for a mysterious three-letter space after the puzzling word *spokes*. When he gingerly asked the girl to explain, she replied quietly that she belonged to a group that had vowed never to type in full the words *chairman, spokesman* and the like. Does the embargo extend to *woman*?

No one denies that words are powerful symbols of feeling and attitude and, as such, solid parts of the social structure. That is why from time to time it seems as if to change the structure one need only change the words. The trouble is that language is too subtle, and the force of common speech, set in its course by the generations, sweeps the censor away like a twig in a torrent. Suppose you get rid of *chairman* and *spokesman* by dint of not typing them. What will you do with *minuteman* or *Frenchman?* "Paul Revere was a minuteperson." Honestly!

Person is not a word to cherish. In mid-career at Rome, it certainly had associations with the emptiness of a mask—*persona*. In French, indeed, it often means *nobody:* "Who's there?"—*"Personne."* Who does not feel that in its ano-nymity the word is disagreeably hoity-toity: "There is a person at the door"? Sound and length unsuit it for spon-taneous use in dozens of ordinary places: "Yes, it's a person-made lake." "She had to be personhandled to break up the quarrel." If English is thus in need of revision and reform, the task ahead is formidable. Must *man-of-war* be *warper-son?*

Within the great treasury of terms and their combina-tions, all of us equal and emancipated human beings must accept the rough with the smooth. We must understand that the "brotherhood of man" does not exclude our beloved sisters; that the potent formula Liberty, Equality, Fraternity cannot be revised to end with either Sorority or Personality; that *mankind* in modern usage is not the opposite of *wom-ankind;* that we are all *fellowman* and *fellowmen* together.

Even if all the women typists of the world should with-hold the last syllable of *spokesman*, their success would hardly legislate the reforms they are after. Important goals must be fought for on their own grounds. Demand equal pay for equal work and the world will come to it.

I conclude, on the source of history and etymology, that "Madam chairman" is a correct and decent appellation. The *man* in it denotes either sex, and therefore the key word means precisely *chairperson*. For my part, I shall continue to use it unless stopped by the chair herself—or a chair itself.

Watch Your Language!

BY THEODORE M. BERNSTEIN

Can you spot the misused word in this sentence: "After a series of fits and starts the stock market eked out a gain."? For years the late Theodore Bernstein, assistant managing editor of the New York Times, campaigned for better writing in a peppery house organ called Winners & Sinners. Here are extracts. And what did Bernstein find wrong with that sentence about the stock market? See his remarks about "eke" below.

AMID, AMONG. *"Firemen groped among the wreckage."*

"Among" means in the midst of countable things. When the things are not separable, the word is "amid" or "amidst."

AS WELL AS. *"He, as well as the producer, are Broadway newcomers."*

"As well as" is a subordinating, not a coördinating, conjunction; it is not the equivalent of "and." Therefore, its

73

presence does not make the subject plural. The sentence should read, ". . . is a Broadway newcomer."

CIRCLE. *"Thousands had circled around the bier."*
Strike out "around."

CLIMAX. *"The drop in popularity of the larger engine reached its climax last September."*

"Climax," which comes from a Greek word meaning ladder, refers to an ascending series. A low point cannot be a climax.

CONCLAVE. *"Secret Conclave Winds Up Discussion."*

The word "conclave" (based on the Latin "clavis," meaning key) originally referred to a room that could be locked, and now means a secret or private meeting. "Secret" is redundant; therefore, omit it.

CONVINCE. *"Three persons tried to convince her to take her seat on the plane."*

"Persuade" would be the proper word in this construction. "Convince" may be followed by an "of" phrase or a "that" clause, but not by a "to" infinitive. "Convince" has the meaning of satisfy beyond doubt by appealing to reason. "Persuade" has the meaning of inducing or winning over by appealing to reason and feeling.

EKE. *"After a series of fits and starts the stock market eked out a gain."*

"Eke" has Anglo-Saxon roots meaning to increase or add. When you eke something out, you add to it or supplement it. What is eked out is not the thing that results but the original stock or supply. In short, "eke out" does not mean "squeeze out," as the quoted sentence suggests.

END RESULT. *"The end result of segregation and lack of compulsory education for Africans . . ."*

An end result is conceivable in the working out of a mathematical problem in which there are intermediate results, but in everyday English an end result is simply a result.

IN TERMS OF. The phrase "in terms of" has a fine, learned sound. But usually it signifies nothing. "He could not have been thinking in terms of the job he was to take." What is meant here is *"about* the job."

INTO. *"He dived in the river and swam in the direction of the woman."*

If he dived in the river, he was already in the water before he performed the action; "in" denotes merely position. The required word here is "into."

LOCATED. *"The canyon is located about 60 miles northwest."*

To locate is to find or fix the position of something. The use of "located" for "situated" is a catachresis. Often, as in the example cited, no word at all is necessary.

MUTUAL. *"Their mutual interest in guns has provided an informal means of instructing youngsters."*

"Mutual" has the connotation of reciprocal: If Jones respects Smith and Smith respects Jones they have a mutual respect. However, if Jones and Smith are both interested in guns, that is not a mutual but a common interest.

PODIUM. *"President Ayub gripped the podium as he answered questions."*

Toehold? A podium is a platform or dais that you stand on or sit on. Therefore you don't grip it, as you would a lectern.

REITERATE. *"Dr. Brode reiterated the suggestion he made last December."*

"Iterate," which is not in general use, means to say or do a second time or often; "reiterate" means, therefore, to say or do over and over again. "Repeat" or "restate" is the better word for a first echo.

REPULSE. *"Some students are repulsed by the thought of going into debt for an education."*

To be repulsed is to be beaten or driven back. The desired word is "repelled," which conveys the idea of aversion.

TROVE. *"A Pre-Inca Trove Is Found in Peru."*

Know what a trove is? It's something that's found.

VIA. *"Attack would entail simultaneous delivery, via missiles or bombers, of nuclear weapons."*

"Via" means by way of (in a geographical sense), not by means of.

Word Power Test No. 7

To Look and Dance and Read and Listen

BY PETER FUNK

These words come from current reviews of movies, theater, dance, books and music. If some of the words are new to you, take one or two each day and use them. A lawyer gave me the secret of his rich vocabulary: "I deliberately overuse a word for a few days, and that helps me to remember it." Select the word or phrase *nearest in meaning* to the key word. Answers appear at the end of this test.

1. **protégé** (prō′ tuh zhā)—A: original thinker. B: heir. C: one who is helped by another. D: mentor.
2. **ingénue** (an zhā noō′)—A: apprentice. B: clever person. C: naïve girl. D: dowager.
3. **quotidian** (kwō tid′ ē un)—A: daily. B: shared. C: measured. D: repetitious.
4. **premier** (prī mir′, -myir′; prē′ mē ur)—A: most important. B: inconspicuous. C: splendid. D: unspoiled.
5. **plaudit** (plaw′ dit)—A: commonplace statement. B: gracious response. C: incisive question. D: enthusiastic approval.
6. **grotesque** (grō tesk′)—A: symmetrical. B: bizarre. C: unforgivable. D: strong.
7. **callow** (kal ō)—A: tough. B: inexperienced. C: superficial. D: sickly.
8. **swivet** (swiv′ ut)—A: agitation. B: repose. C: connection. D: tiny animal.
9. **egocentric** (ē gō sen′ trik)—A: peculiar. B: self-centered. C: limited. D: circular.
10. **prehensile** (prī hen′ s′l)—Formed to A: coil around anything. B: stretch. C: aid in survival. D: produce energy.
11. **imprecation** (im pruh kā′ shun)—A: threat. B: curse. C: consequence. D: benediction.

12. **blather** (blath′ ur)—A: to tell a secret. B: talk foolishly. C: cry noisily. D: gossip.

13. **pedantry** (ped′ ′n trē)—A: irritating slowness. B: ostentatious display of learning. C: sound judgment. D: ignorance.

14. **bogus** (bō′ gus)—A: false. B: inferior. C: spooky. D: extra.

15. **posit** (pŏz′ it)—A: to baffle. B: displace. C: assume. D: discover.

16. **gull**—A: to soothe. B: soar. C: dream. D: deceive.

17. **surrogate** (sur′ uh gāt)—A: substitute. B: accused. C: authenticated. D: protected.

18. **moment** (mō′ munt)—A: concurrence. B: importance. C: clarity. D: quickness.

19. **bibulous** (bib′ ū lus)—A: humorous. B: officious. C: addicted to alcohol. D: garrulous.

20. **inordinately** (in or′ d′n it lē)—A: rarely. B: unexpectedly. C: excessively. D: unsuitably.

ANSWERS

1. **protégé**—C: One whose career is helped by another more influential person. Latin *protegere* (to protect). "The young actor became the director's *protégé*."

2. **ingénue**—C: An actress playing the role of a naïve, innocent or inexperienced girl. French *ingénu* (unsophisticated).

3. **quotidian**—A: Daily; recurring each day, especially whatever is ordinary; as, to record *quotidian* experiences. Latin *quotidianus,* from *quotidie* (daily).

4. **premier**—A: Most important; foremost. French from Latin *primarius* (of the first rank). "He ranked as Germany's *premier* conductor."

5. **plaudit**—D: Any enthusiastic expression of approval or praise; as, "He won *plaudits* for his dancing." Latin *plaudite,* literally a request for applause (clap your hands!) from *plaudere* (to applaud).

6. **grotesque**—B: Bizarre. Old Italian *grottesca* (cave painting).

7. **callow**—B: Inexperienced; immature; resembling young birds lacking flying features; as a *callow* musician. Old English *calu* (bald).

8. **swivet**—A: State of agitation or annoyance. "The TV pro-

ducers are in a *swivet* about the Emmy awards." Origin unknown.

9. **egocentric**—B: Self-centered; evaluating everything only in relation to oneself; as, a difficult, *egocentric* artist. Latin *ego* (I) and *centrum* (center).

10. **prehensile**—A: Formed to coil around or grasp hold of— as a tail, hand or, metaphorically, the mind. "Retailers eye *King Kong's* potential with *prehensile* enthusiasm." Latin *prehendere* (to seize).

11. **imprecation**—B: Curse; vengeful wish that a calamity befall another. Latin *imprecatio* (act of praying).

12. **blather**—B: To talk in a foolish, babbling way; as, "The characters acted like *blathering* romantic idiots." Old Norse *blathr*.

13. **pedantry**—B: Ostentatious or boring display of learning and slavish attention to unnecessary details. Italian *pedanteria*.

14. **bogus**—A: False; not genuine; as, *bogus* revelations about the political system. (Originally an apparatus for making counterfeit money.)

15. **posit**—C: To assume; affirm something is true; as, "Saul Bellow *posits* the importance of the novel." Latin *positus* (placed, put).

16. **gull**—D: To deceive, trick or defraud; as, "He has been *gulled* into dating Carrie." Perhaps from dialectical *gull* (young bird, silly fellow).

17. **surrogate**—A: Substitute; having the authority to act for another; as, "They filled the role of *surrogate* parents." Latin *surrogatus*.

18. **moment**—B: Importance; having outstanding significance, consequence, or value; as, a publishing event of great *moment*. Latin *momentum* (movement).

19. **bibulous**—C: Latin *bibulus* means fond of drinking; hence, a *bibulous* adventurer is one addicted to drink.

20. **inordinately**—C: Excessively; immoderately; as, "The artist Cézanne became *inordinately* timid." Latin *inordinatus* (disorderly).

VOCABULARY RATINGS

20—19 correct ....exceptional
18—15 correct ....excellent
14—12 correct .... good

How To Argue

The best way is to listen

BY STUART CHASE

Suppose a stranger tries to pick a quarrel with you, at a cocktail party, let us say, or a conference. He comes up and says: "I hear you like labor unions; well, they are nothing but a lot of rackets!"

Suppose further that you have a long and honorable record as an impartial student of labor problems, which makes this pretty close to an insult. What are you going to do?

There are three obvious things to do—and one not so obvious. You can hit him. You can turn your back and walk away with as much dignity as you can summon. You can say: "You don't know what you're talking about!" and start a slam-bang argument. This will probably draw a crowd like a soapbox debate, and like such debates it will get precisely nowhere.

These are the normal courses of action, but this time, in the interests of peace, and of science, suppose you try an experiment. Stand your ground, put on as reasonable an expression as can be mustered, and say nothing at all.

Your man looks surprised, but soon rallies to the attack: "Pegler is dead right when he says unions are all run by racketeers!"

You continue to keep your foot hard on the brake. The essence of the experiment is to refuse to argue on big general statements, where nobody knows what the other fellow means. "Well," you say, "that's one point of view. Tell me some more."

Your man blinks and clears his throat. He is plainly disconcerted. "Well—er—Pegler ought to know, oughtn't he?" Now he is moving from offensive to defensive. If you are tempted to follow up the advantage, resist the temptation.

"Go ahead," you say, "I'm listening." And you *are* listening. You are trying to determine what makes him act this way. Did a labor union once give him a rough deal? Or what?

Your man opens his mouth, closes it, and goes into neutral. "Well, some people think they're rackets; what do you think?" This is the signal that the experiment has been successful! The attack has fizzled out. The man who came to back you into a corner is now asking your opinion. You can leave him disarmed, or you can continue the experiment. Suppose you tell him about a case of racketeering which you personally investigated. "A very bad business." (You have saved his face by admitting he has a case; some unions are indeed rackets.) "But now take the Amalgamated Clothing Workers, who even endorse bank loans sometimes to employers who are in trouble. One could hardly call that racketeering?"

Since you have listened to him, he is now willing to listen to you. He admits that the Amalgamated is a responsible union. He admits that he may be a little prejudiced. You can then discuss various other cases without emotion, on their merits. Both of you learn something which neither of you knew before. No fisticuffs, no enemies, no shouting, and no backing down on your part.

This ingenious technique was first outlined to me by S. I. Hayakawa. I have used it on a number of occasions with considerable success.

The essence is in *listening*. Don't hit, don't contradict, don't cave in or turn the other cheek. Just say: "Tell me some more, I'm listening."

Bernard Shaw once said that the degree of emotion in

a controversy varies inversely with knowledge of the subject. And usually the offensive does have very few facts with which to back up its emotion! (I find that most attackers run out of gas in about three minutes.)

When you accept your attacker as a human being with a legitimate point of view, his self-confidence is not threatened; he will eventually try to find out what *you* think, and may go quite a way to agree with you.

Thank You,
William Shakespeare!

BY GUY WRIGHT

I doubt that there's anyone reading this who goes through a normal day's conversation without quoting Shakespeare. Once in a while we realize we're doing this, but most of the time we lift his lines to season our speech and sharpen our opinions without the slightest thought of the source.*

When you call a man a "rotten apple," a "blinking idiot" or a "popinjay" . . . When you say he "bears a charmed life" or is "hoist with his own petard" . . . When you proclaim him "a man of few words" . . .

When you speak of "cold comfort," "grim necessity," "bag and baggage," the "mind's eye," "holding your tongue," "suiting the action to the words" . . . When you refer to your "salad days" or "heart of hearts" . . . When you deplore "the beginning of the end," "life's uncertain voyage" or "the unkindest cut of all" . . .

*Some of the expressions have changed a bit with everyday usage, but even these can be easily traced to the master.

By golly, you're quoting Shakespeare!

When you use such expressions as "poor but honest," "one fell swoop," "as luck would have it," "the short and the long of it," "neither here nor there," "what's done is done" . . .

When you say something "smells to heaven" or is "Greek to me," or it's a "mad world" or "not in my book" . . .

When you complain that you "haven't slept a wink" or that your family is "eating you out of house and home," or you've "seen better days" . . .

When you speak of a coward "showing his heels" or having "no stomach for a fight" . . .

When you nod wisely and say, "Love is blind" . . . or "Truth will come to light" . . . or "The world is my oyster" . . .

You are borrowing your *bon mot* from the Bard. Shakespeare was the greatest cliché inventor of all time. Without him to put the words in our mouths, we would be virtually tongue-tied, and the English language would have a lean and hungry look.

Word Power Test No. 8

Nouns—Airborne and Not

BY PETER FUNK

Nouns can stay down to earth, or they can fly. They can embody the substantial thing—house, chair, car. Or they can take wing and capture abstractions—freedom, affection, faith. The following 20 nouns are of both kinds: the earthbound and the airborne, the concrete and the abstract. Check the word or phrase that you believe is *nearest in meaning* to the key word. Answers appear at the end of this test.

1. **sensibility** (sen sĭ bil′ ĭ tē)—A: tenderness. B: daintiness. C: impracticality. D: sensitivity.
2. **irruption** (ĭ rup′ shun)—A: interference. B: altercation. C: a bursting in. D: hiatus.
3. **procrastination** (pro krăs tĭ nā′ shun)—A: prediction. B: uncertainty. C: postponement. D: harshness.
4. **array** (ă rā′)—A: impressive display. B: mixture. C: variety. D: kaleidoscope.
5. **token**—A: symbol. B: attempt. C: clue. D: suggestion.
6. **malfunction** (mal funk′ shun)—A: change. B: mistake. C: defect. D: difference.
7. **windfall**—A: row of bushes and trees. B: calm. C: gale. D: good fortune.
8. **crotchet** (krŏtch′ it)—A: gear box. B: forked junction. C: valise. D: eccentricity.
9. **denizen** (den′ ĭ zĕn)—A: inhabitant. B: fugitive. C: debtor. D: poet.
10. **largess** (lar jĕs′)—A: bulkiness. B: exaggeration. C: generosity. D: grandiloquence.
11. **rubric** (rōō′ brik)—A: proverb. B: oddity. C: ruralism. D: instruction.

12. **leeway** (lē′ wā)—A: leisure. B: permissiveness. C: course. D: flexibility.

13. **perimeter** (pĕ rim′ ĕ ter)—A: outer boundary. B: proportion. C: zone. D: parade ground.

14. **symbiosis** (sim bī ō′ sis)—A: isolation. B: mutual dependence. C: compromise. D: representation.

15. **euphemism** (ū′ fĕ mis'm)—A: praise. B: inoffensive expression. C: cheerfulness. D: prudery.

16. **allegiance** (ă lē′ jans)—A: worship. B: loyalty. C: respect. D: friendship.

17. **humility** (hū mil′ ĭ tē)—A: modesty. B: hauteur. C: embarrassment. D: deviousness.

18. **animosity** (an ĭ mŏs′ ĭ tē)—A: active resistance. B: liveliness. C: concord. D: strong dislike.

19. **extravaganza** (ek străv ă gan′ za)—A: spectacular show. B: falsification. C: profligacy. D: over-reaching.

20. **credentials** (krĭ den′ shalz)—A: testimonials. B: talents. C: compliments. D: beliefs.

ANSWERS

1. **sensibility**—D: Sensitivity; awareness; the capacity to be strongly moved emotionally. Latin *sensibilis* (perceptive, intelligent).

2. **irruption**—C: An explosive bursting or rushing in; as, an *irruption* of vandals into city schools. Latin *irrumpere* (to break in).

3. **procrastination**—C: Postponement; habitually putting off or delaying. One who is guilty of *procrastination* makes his work a matter "for tomorrow." Latin *procrastinatus; pro* (forward) and *cras* (tomorrow).

4. **array**—A: An impressive display of people or objects; an orderly grouping. Medieval Latin *arredare* (to put in order).

5. **token**—A: Symbol or sign of authenticity. A gift may be a *token* of friendship. Old English *tacen* (to provide with means of identification).

6. **malfunction**—C: Defect; failure to function in the usual way. French *mal* and *function*.

7. **windfall**—D: Sudden profit or good fortune. Old English *wind* and *fall*—i.e., ripe fruit blown down by the wind.

8. **crotchet**—D: An eccentricity; stubborn notion; as, "If you

have a *crotchet* about stuffy rooms, you probably sleep with a window open." Old French *crochet* (a small hook).

9. **denizen**—A: Inhabitant or habitual visitor; as, "The red-wing blackbird is a *denizen* of swamps." Old French *denzein* (native inhabitant).

10. **largess**—C: Generosity; often the ostentatious giving of gifts; as, the *largess* of Washington lobbyists. Old French *large* (generous).

11. **rubric**—D: Instruction; brief commentary; custom; ecclesiastical rule. Latin *ruber* (red). Medieval monks used red ink for headings in prayer books.

12. **leeway**—D: Flexibility; latitude; additional time or space; as, *leeway* of an extra week to complete a job.

13. **perimeter**—A: Outer boundary of an area; as, the *perimeter* of a circle. Greek *peri* (around) and *metron* (measure).

14. **symbiosis**—B: Mutual dependence between different organisms. Greek *symbiosis* (living together).

15. **euphemism**—B: An inoffensive expression; roundabout word substituted for another to avoid giving offense. "He passed away" is a *euphemism* for "he died." Greek *euphemizein* (to speak favorably).

16. **allegiance**—B: Loyalty to a government, person, cause. Old French *ligeance* (obligations of a serf to his master, or *liege*).

17. **humility**—A: Modesty; as, "St. Francis of Assisi exemplified *humility*, for he was free of arrogance and was self-effacing." Latin *humus* (earth).

18. **animosity**—D: Having a strong dislike; as, "The *animosity* between the two hockey teams led to a brawl." Latin *animositas* (high spirits).

19. **extravaganza**—A: A spectacular and elaborate show. Italian *estravaganza* (extravagance).

20. **credentials**—A: Testimonials; evidence of one's qualifications; as, a doctor's medical *credentials*. Latin *credentialis* (giving authority).

VOCABULARY RATINGS

20—19 correct ....exceptional
18—15 correct ....excellent
14—12 correct .... good

Alphabet You'll Like These Puns

BY JOHN S. CROSBIE

But only the reader can judge. Are these plays on words fair or foul? Do they add up to a cruel—or sleight—sentence of punishment?

AARDVARK: Heavy labor: "It's aardvark, but it pays well."

AMAZON: "You can pay for the eggs, but the Amazon me."

BACKWARD: Hospital section for sacroiliac cases.

BIGAMIST: Italian fog.

BUDGIE: Mother's whistler.

CACHE: In desperation, the Czechoslovakian midget pounded on his friend's door. "The Russian police are after

me!" he cried. "Can't you please cache a small Czech?"
CATGUT: Our dog got fleas, but our catgut kittens.

DAIS: When the platform collapsed in the middle of his lecture, the professor picked himself up, sighed and said, "Some dais are like that!"

DUET: Pity the man who couldn't find anyone to sing with! He went out and bought a duet yourself kit.

EARL: When his lordship's crew mutinied during a storm, they poured the earl on the troubled waters.

EDIFICE: Sign on a junkyard fence: "Edifice wrecks."

FAULT: After a major earthquake in northern California, a group of concerned citizens set up the San Andreas Fund, proving that Californians can be generous to a fault.

GALLEON: Before cars were invented, Spaniards were able to go for thousands of miles on a galleon.

HEARSE: The undertaker ordered a new vehicle—in light blue, this time. He thought it time to try a hearse of a different color.

HIMALAYA: "Yesterday was Father's birthday so Mother made Himalaya cake."

IGLOO: Material used to keep an ig from falling apart.
INCONGRUOUS: Where U.S. laws are made.
INFIDEL: The Vatican is not inclined to believe infidel Castro.

JOYCE, JAMES: "Last night I chose to read a new book; it turned out to be an unfortunate Joyce."

KERCHIEF: *Gesundheit!*

LAPSE: What we get when we sit down.
LATH: In choosing a carpenter to install laths, always pick a slow and careful man because he whose laths last, laths best.

MACHIAVELLI: I know a tailor who will Machiavelli good pair of pants for $30.

MEDICATION: The guru refused to let his dentist freeze his jaw because he wanted to transcend dental medication.

MELANCHOLY: A dog that won't eat anything but cantaloupes.

MENAGERIE: The equator is a menagerie lion running around the earth.

NEWT: He was really a salamander but no one newt.

NICHOLAS: "But, Joe, I can't marry you. You're penniless." "That's nothing, the Tsar of Russia was Nicholas."

OPPORTUNE: Any well-known operatic melody.

PACE: Male jogger to female jogger: "My pace or yours?"

PARANOIA: One mental-hospital patient to another, pointing to the two psychiatrists doing ward rounds: "Don't let that paranoia."

QUART: People who drink before they drive are putting the quart before the hearse.

REBATE: Put another worm on the hook.

RINGLEADER: The first one in the bathtub.

SHED: As the critic wrote of the stripper: "Some things are better left unshed."

TEUTONIC: Not enough gin.

THESIS: Professor's cryptic comment on a returned college essay: "Thesis awful."

THONGS: What Thinatra things.

URN: Q. What's a Grecian urn? A. Oh, about 20 drachmas a week after taxes.

VERSE: Just remember—no matter how bad these puns may be, they could be verse!

WANTON: The miniskirt was tried and found wanton.

XENOPHON: How Cyrus the Younger kept in touch with home office.

YEW: "I cedar hedge is growing." "Yes, it's all up to yew."

ZINC: The battery would not have been invented if someone hadn't stopped to zinc.

ZINNIA: The florid American farewell: "I'll be zinnia!"

Anything Goes, Verbalizationwise

CONDENSED FROM NEWSWEEK

It used to be called gobbledygook, or just plain double-talk. Now it has achieved the status of a fine art.

Once confined to Madison Avenue and Foggy Bottom, jargon, euphemisms, circumlocutions and other high-flown forms of linguistic obfuscation have now become as pervasive as pollution. From San Antonio "people express-ways" (sidewalks) to New York City (where a garage mechanic advertises himself as an "automotive internist"), the word is out that anything goes, verbalizationwise.

Physicians are starting to call pep pills "activity boosters." Preschoolers are now enrolled in "early-learning centers," where they orbit between their "pupil stations" (desks) and the "instructional materials resource center" (library). In a letter to shareholders, Litton Industries attributed a decline in profits to "volume variances from plan" (strikes).

Much of the word pollution results from a tropistic reaction to a disagreeable truth. This creates a growing need for sugar-coated palliatives. Vietnam popularized "gradualism," "infrastructure" and "defoliation," while prompting one State Department official to suggest that U.S. bombing pressure on the enemy "should be mainly violins, but with periodic touches of brass" (more selective than massive). British satirist David Frost is a veteran observer of the genre. As he sees it, the term "strategic withdrawal" usually means a rout; a "phased withdrawal" is a rout with insufficient transport.

Nowhere has the art of obfuscation been more refined than in the drawing up of administrative proposals. An officer for the New York City Planning Commission says the cardinal rule is never to mention money. "'Resources' is the prime substitute, although 'allocations' and 'appropriations' are also popular. 'Resources' is also esthetically pleasing, because it suggests the act of digging up and forms a truly Miltonic phrase when preceded by 'overburdened municipal.'"

A second rule is to fluff up a proposal with the sort of euphemisms that bestow an aura of importance without revealing anything specific. An application from a small southern California college for a federal grant states: "It is not simply a cross-disciplinary venture or an interdisciplinary venture; it is a pandisciplinary venture and this, of course, is the nature of all real experience."

Even the high priests of the newtime religion play the game, especially when they are called on for personal commitments. As theologian Robert McAfee Brown notes, leading statements like "I believe . . ." have given way to the more anonymous "The Judeo-Christian tradition affirms . . ."

Only the Supreme Deity knows where it will all be finalized—or, for that matter, what it all means.

HOW TO WIN AT WORDSMANSHIP

After years of hacking through etymological thickets at the U.S. Public Health Service, a 63-year-old official named Philip Broughton hit upon a sure-fire method for converting frustration into fulfillment (jargonwise). Euphemistically called the Systematic Buzz Phrase Projector, Broughton's system employs a lexicon of 30 carefully chosen "buzzwords":

Column 1	Column 2	Column 3
0. integrated	0. management	0. options
1. total	1. organizational	1. flexibility
2. systematized	2. monitored	2. capability
3. parallel	3. reciprocal	3. mobility
4. functional	4. digital	4. programming
5. responsive	5. logistical	5. concept
6. optional	6. transitional	6. time-phase
7. synchronized	7. incremental	7. projection
8. compatible	8. third-generation	8. hardware
9. balanced	9. policy	9. contingency

The procedure is simple. Think of any three-digit number, then select the corresponding buzzword from each column. For instance, number 257 produces "systematized logistical projection," a phrase that can be dropped into virtually any report with that ring of decisive, knowledgeable authority. "No one will have the remotest idea of what you're talking about," says Broughton. "But the important thing is that they're not about to admit it."

Word Power Test No. 9

Living Latin

BY PETER FUNK

Far from being a dead language, Latin lives in a high proportion of English words, but often in disguised form. The 20 words in this test have come down to us from the days of Caesar virtually unchanged in spelling or meaning. And so have many others. Even such commonly encountered words as senator, campus, liquor, pastor and animal—all exactly the same as the Latin—confirm what an enduring element it is in our modern usage. Check the word or phrase *nearest in meaning*. Answers appear at the end of this test.

1. **placebo** (pluh sē′ bō)—A: familiar location. B: hideaway. C: peace offering. D: harmless pill.
2. **status** (stā′ tus; stă′ tus)—A: position. B: legislation. C: edict. D: fashion.
3. **opus** (ō′ pus)—A: legal document. B: garden tool. C: a particular procedure. D: work or composition.
4. **non sequitur** (non sĕk′ wĭ tur)—A: demand. B: limit. C: irrelevant remark. D: without influence.
5. **latitude** (lăt′ ĭ tūde)—A: diversity of opinion. B: time zone. C: range or scope. D: periphery.
6. **opprobrium** (ŏ prō′ brē um)—A: praise. B: burden. C: cruelty. D: disgrace.
7. **ultra**—A: noteworthy. B: different. C: excessive. D: negligible.
8. **terminus** (tur′ mĭ nus)—A: short period of time. B: finishing point. C: starting point. D: interruption.
9. **detritus** (dē trī′ tus)—A: scaffolding. B: race track. C: alternate route. D: debris.
10. **tuber** (tū′ ber)—A: swollen root. B: musical instrument. C: measuring tool. D: greeting.

94

11. **tedium** (tē′ dē um)—A: excitement. B: nostalgia. C: paradox. D: boredom.

12. **de facto** (dē făk′ tō)—A: actual. B: stopgap. C: dated. D: unfounded.

13. **radius** (rā′ dē us)—A: type of curve. B: beam of light. C: distance from a center to the edge. D: radioactive mineral.

14. **impetus** (im′ pě tus)—A: oversight. B: stimulus. C: impatience. D: hindrance.

15. **mores** (mor′ āz; mor′ ēz)—A: germs. B. descendants. C: apologies. D: customs.

16. **regimen** (rěj′ ǐ men)—A: political faction. B: body of troops. C: dictatorship. D: systematic approach to health.

17. **interim** (in′ ter im)—A: eternal. B: temporary. C: timely. D: open.

18. **nominal** (nom′ ǐ n′l)—A: having a name in common. B: in name only. C: pertaining to an average. D: gradually changing.

19. **clamor** (klăm′ or)—A: dampness. B: outcry. C: conciliation. D: disorder.

20. **nonplus**—A: to dumfound. B: anger. C: withdraw. D: be neutral.

ANSWERS

1. **placebo**—D: Harmless pill; as, "The patient did not know his pill was merely a *placebo*." Literally, "I shall please."

2. **status**—A: A person's relative position in society measured by wealth, prestige, standing; as, "The award enhanced the musician's *status*." Also, a condition or situation; as, to report on the *status* of trade negotiations.

·3. **opus**—D: A work or composition, especially in music and numbered in the order of publication; as, Chopin's Prelude, *opus* 28, number 16.

4. **non sequitur**—C: Literally, "It does not follow"; therefore, an irrelevant remark, or a conclusion that does not follow from the evidence; as, "It is a *non sequitur* to relate the number of cats and dogs to the rainfall."

5. **latitude**—C: Range or scope; a wide variety of choices; as, to be allowed *latitude* in behavior and dress.

6. **opprobrium**—D: Disgrace; dishonor brought about by shameful conduct; as, "He resigned from the Presidency under a cloud of *opprobrium*."

7. **ultra**—C: Excessive in the extreme; going beyond the normal limits or range; as, an *ultra* liberal.

8. **terminus**—B: Finishing point; goal; terminal; as, "The airline *terminus* was London."

9. **detritus**—D: Debris; accumulation of disintegrated material; as, "Leaves, branches . . . this *detritus* gets mixed with the soil on the forest floor."

10. **tuber**—A: Swollen, fleshy root; potato; as, "This homely *tuber*—the potato—is the world's most important vegetable."

11. **tedium**—D: Boredom; monotony; as, "CB radio is widely used to relieve freeway *tedium*."

12. **de facto**—A: Actual; in reality; as, a *de facto* government.

13. **radius**—C: Distance from a center of a circle to the edge; as, three lakes within a *radius* of five miles. (Spoke of a wheel.)

14. **impetus**—B: Stimulus to activity; driving force; as, "Reggie Jackson's enthusiasm is an *impetus* for the team."

15. **mores**—D: The traditional customs, manners and morals of a group or community; as, the *mores* of the Kentucky mountain people.

16. **regimen**—D: Systematic manner of living to improve or maintain one's health by diet, exercise, routine; as, the *regimen* of a professional athlete.

17. **interim**—B: An *interim* job or committee is temporary, provisional or for the time.

18. **nominal**—B: In name only; not actually true or real; as, a *nominal* leader; also, very slight or insignificant; as, a *nominal* price.

19. **clamor**—B: Outcry; shouting; noisy expression of dissent or approval; as, the *clamor* of the angry crowd protesting the new highway route.

20. **nonplus**—A: To dumfound. When we are *nonplused* by a situation, we are so startled that temporarily we are incapable of further action. (*Non* "no" and *plus* "further.")

VOCABULARY RATINGS

20—18 correct ....exceptional
17—15 correct ....excellent
14—12 correct ....good

The Meaning Manglers

BY JAMES THURBER

Something central and essential in the mechanism of meaning began losing its symmetry last summer. At first I thought the fault must be in myself, some flaw of comprehension or concentration, aggravated by the march of time. Then I realized one June afternoon at a cocktail party in Bermuda that the trouble was largely female, or at least seemed to originate in that sex, like so many other alarming things.

At this party, a woman from the Middle West began telling me about some legal involvement her daughter and son-in-law had got into. She ended her cloudy recital on a note of triumph. "So finally they decided to leave it where sleeping dogs lie," she said.

I was upon it in a moment. "How perfectly charming of them both, dear lady," I cried. "One can only hope the barristers for the other side will tumble for it, hook, line and barrel. To be sure, they may overtake it in their stride, in which case may the devil pay the hindmost."

Upon this my companion cautiously withdrew to the safer company of younger minds.

The charmingly tainted idiom of the lady of the sleeping dogs must have infected other members of her circle, among them a beautiful young woman who told me, "We are not going to hide our heads in the sand like kangaroos." This twisted and inspired simile was just what my harassed understanding and tortured spirits needed. Whenever I think I hear the men coming with the stretcher or the subpoena, I remember those kangaroos with their strange and enormous rear quarters protruding from the earth, and I am ready to face anything again.

It was only a fortnight later, at a cocktail party in New York, that the proud mother of a young man who had just completed his first year as a history teacher sat down beside me and leaped into a discussion of history professors in general. "It is not easy to make them colleagues," she said. "They are always looking down each other's noses."

I let my awareness deal with this troubled idiom for a long moment before replying. "At least," I said, "when there is so much smoke one knows one is in Denmark. But be of good cheer. I can fairly see the butter melting in their mouths now."

Ours is a precarious language, as every writer knows, in which the merest shadow line often separates sense from nonsense. One linotyper became co-author of a piece of mine by introducing a bear into the story. He simply made one out of a bead that was lying around in the middle of the narrative. This set me to brooding, and for weeks I lay awake at night playing unhappily with imaginary havoc wrought by single-letter changes in the printed word: "A stitch in time saves none. . . . There's no business like shoe business. . . . Lafayette, we ate here. . . . Don, give up the ship."

In Martha's Vineyard last August—is there something about islands that fogs the clarity of speech?—I fell into conversation with an actress I had known in my Greenwich Village or devil-may-care days, and we began counting our Village friends of 30 years ago. One, it turned out, was still living in the same old place. "Her apartment was broken into so often, she finally had to have it burglarized," my friend told me.

My aging mind had to turn that over several times. "You

mean there's a *company* that burglarizes apartments now?" I finally demanded. "What do you do—call them up and tell them when you won't be home?"

My companion eyed me warily. "You don't have to not be home," she said.

"Most people are not home when their apartments are burglarized," I told her. "Are you sure she didn't have the place just alarmed?"

"I don't know what you're talking about," said my old friend, moving away.

I am back at my home in Connecticut now. Our community in the foothills of the Berkshires wears a special radiance in the person of a French lady whom I shall call Renée. Renée is mistress of what I call not the dangling participle but the dazzling participle, often, when excited, using it in place of the past tense.

"How did you like the concert at Tanglewood last night?" I asked her one day.

"I was fascinating," she said.

Renée is always fascinating. She is a social critic, too, and I am a fond collector of some of her rarer pronouncements, of which my favorite is this: "The womans are stronger at the bottom."

Some 15 years ago, our usually tranquil community was violently upset by the attempted murder of a woman. The state police questioned us all, and did not come off very well with Renée.

"One thing I am certain of," a detective said to her. "Somebody in this town is guilty."

"So am I," said the innocent and wonderful Renée.

The cop stared at her. "Where do you live?" he asked.

Renée, who was standing on her front porch, waved a hand at her house and said, "I am leaving here."

The harassed police officer gave her another long and rueful look, sighed, and said, "So am I," and went away.

Why Johnny Can't Write

BY MERRILL SHEILS

If your children are attending college, the chances are that when they graduate they will be unable to write ordinary, expository English with any real degree of structure and lucidity. If they are in high school and planning to attend college, the chances are less than even that they will be able to write English at the minimal college level when they get there. If they are not planning to attend college, their skills in writing English may not even qualify them for secretarial or clerical work. And if they are attending elementary school, they are almost certainly not being given the kind of required reading material, much less writing instruction, that might make it possible for them eventually to write comprehensible English. Willy-nilly, the U.S. educational system is spawning a generation of semi-literates.

Nationwide, the statistics on both reading and writing grow more appalling each year. The United States, says poet Karl Shapiro, "is in the midst of a literary breakdown." Historian Jacques Barzun concludes, "We have ceased to think with words."

The evidence is massive. Firms seeking secretaries who can spell and punctuate, or junior executives who can write intelligible reports, complain that college graduates no longer fill the bill. "Errors we once found in applications from high-school graduates are now cropping up in forms from people with four-year-college degrees," says a personnel official for the Bank of America. At the University of California at Berkeley, where students come from the top 12.5 percent of high-school graduates, nearly half of last year's freshmen were so seriously deficient at organizing their thoughts on paper that they were forced to enroll in remedial courses nicknamed "bonehead English." And when the Association of American Publishers prepared a pamphlet to help college freshmen get the most from their textbooks, it had to be rewritten from a twelfth-grade level to a ninth-grade level so that students could understand it.

DOWN THE TUBE. The breakdown in writing has been in the making for years. The causes range from inadequate grounding in the basics of syntax, structure and style to the popularity of secondary-school curriculums that no longer require the wide range of reading all students must have if they are to learn to write clearly. Educators emphatically agree that a student who cannot read with true comprehension will never learn to write well. "Writing is, after all, book-talk," says Ramon Veal, associate professor of language education at the University of Georgia's College of Education. "You learn book-talk only by reading."

The judges in the National Assessment of Educational Progress study, a panel of English teachers and scholars from across the country, suggest that most people tested have been strongly influenced by the simplistic spoken style of television. E.B. White, *New Yorker* magazine essayist, puts it this way: "Short of throwing away all the television sets, I really don't know what we can do about writing." No one has yet produced a thorough study of the effect of TV on a generation of students raised in its glare, but on at least two points most language experts agree: time spent watching television is time that might otherwise be devoted to reading; and the passiveness of the viewing—"letting the television become one's main environment," in the words of Barzun—seems to have a markedly bad effect on a child's active pursuit of written skills. "The TV keeps children entertained," complains Albert Tillman, director of a writing clinic at the University of Illinois. "It does not demand that they take active part in their learning."

"PRESTIGE" DIALECT. Even the effects of television might be counteracted if students were required to learn the written language in the classroom. There, however, overcrowding and increased workloads have led many teachers to give up assigning essays and to rely, instead, on short-answer exercises that are easier to mark. As a result, many students now graduate from high school without ever having had any real practice in writing.

The 1960s also brought a subtle shift of educational philosophy away from the teaching of expository writing. Many teachers began to emphasize "creativity" in the English classrooms and expanded their curriculums to allow students to work with contemporary media of communication such as film, videotape and photography. Even where writing is still taught, the creative approach discourages insistence on grammar, structure and style, in the belief that rules stifle spontaneity. Elliott Anderson, professor of English at Northwestern University, reports that many high-school teachers have simply stopped correcting poor grammar and sloppy construction.

In the opinion of many language experts, another group of villains are educators who misuse the principles of "structural linguistics." The structural linguists contend that the spoken idiom is superior to the written and that there are no real standards for any language apart from the way it is commonly spoken. Teachers under their influence believe that there is no need for students to study formal language rules. Philologist Mario Pei warns that much of academia is now controlled by those who preach "that the only language activity worthy of the name is speech on the colloquial, slangy, even illiterate plane."

The pervasive influence of the structural linguists, coupled with the political activism of the past decade, has also led many teachers to take the view that standard English is just a "prestige" dialect among many others, and that insistence on its predominance constitutes an act of repression by the white middle class. This attitude ignores the likelihood that students who do not have the opportunity to master standard English will also lose the chance at higher-ranking jobs where standard English does prevail. "Prestige" dialect or not, standard English is in fact the language of American law, politics, commerce and the vast bulk of American literature. To deny children access to it, argue traditionalists, is in itself a pernicious form of oppression.

How to stop the rot in writing skills is a matter of increasingly vigorous debate. The late James Knapton, a former supervisor of remedial English at Berkeley, who quit the university in disgust eight years ago when officials dropped the school's essay requirement for admission, believed that the first step must be to teach the English teachers themselves how to write. Knapton's point is well taken. According to an officer of the National Council of Teachers of English, it is now possible for an aspirant who wants to teach high-school English to go all the way through high school, college and advanced-education degrees without having taken a single course in English composition since the ninth grade.

Some researchers estimate that more than 50 percent of the nation's secondary-school English teachers did not specialize in English at all during their college years. School officials in Maryland were horrified by the results of a recent study which showed that half of the teachers who apply for English-teaching jobs in Montgomery County fail a basic test of grammar, punctuation and spelling.

CLOSING THE GAP. In 1974, educators in San Francisco decided to do something about the teaching gap. The University of California's Berkeley/Bay Area Writing Project invited teachers from nine California counties to spend a five-week summer session with a coalition of Berkeley professors. Five days a week, eight hours a day, the teachers studied current research on writing, examined practical approaches to teaching it, developed curriculum material and wrote extensively on their own. Each then returned to his school district to offer similar training to his colleagues. The workshop was such a success that it was repeated last summer and, as a result, 31 Bay Area school districts have funded their own writing workshops, and a consortium of

California colleges and universities is considering plans for more such programs.

In other areas, a number of schools have come up with their own methods of improving writing skills. At Phillips Academy in Andover, Mass., the traditional four years of required English courses have been replaced with a school-wide requirement for competence in reading and writing. Every student, regardless of his grade level, must take the course—called, simply enough, "Competence"—until he passes it. The premise, says headmaster Theodore Sizer, is elementary: "Until a youngster can demonstrate that he is competent in reading and writing, you just cannot pass him along to more advanced studies."

Television is being appraised as a teaching tool in some places. Since it is here to stay, a number of concerned teachers and researchers are beginning to suggest that it be used to promote—not replace—the study of the written language. "Kids spend three to four hours watching TV every day," says Peter Almond, who has been studying children and television for the Carnegie Council on Children. "Why not learn to use it more wisely?" Almond reports that many of the best teachers already assign reading and writing exercises based on television shows their students watch.

THE RIGHT TO WRITE. Educators agree that it is absolutely essential to make students write. "That's the only way they learn," says Eunice Sims, coördinator of English for the Atlanta school system. "Let them write about whatever interests them and teach from that. You can always move a student from essays on street fighting to essays on Shelley."

Despite the laudable efforts of some individual teachers, however, very little improvement in the writing skills of American students is likely unless the entire educational establishment recaptures the earlier conviction that the written language is important. One thing that is clearly needed is a renewed emphasis on reading as both a discipline and a diversion. Written language—with its fixed, essential rules—remains the only effective vehicle for transmitting and debating a culture's ideas, values and goals. If it is placed at the mercy of every new colloquialism, then we will soon find ourselves back in Babel.

"Learning to write is the hardest, most important thing any child does," says Carlos Baker, professor of English at Princeton University. "Learning to write is learning to think." Adds semanticist S. I. Hayakawa, "You don't know anything clearly unless you can state it in writing."

Word Power Test No. 10

Advertising Words

BY PETER FUNK

Advertisers choose their phrases with skill and great care. The words may come fast but they don't necessarily, or always, come easily. All 20 of the following words were taken from recent advertisements in *Reader's Digest*. Pick the answer you think is right. Answers appear at the end of this test.

1. **invert** (in vert′)—A: to swerve. B: cause to slope. C: turn upside down. D: distract.

2. **redemption** (re demp′ shun)—A: sale. B: gift or contribution. C: protection. D: act of buying back.

3. **console** (cŏn′ sōl)—A: tent. B: merry-go-round. C: cabinet. D: style of car.

4. **parquetry** (par′ kĕ trē)—A: dessert. B: game. C: cast iron. D: inlaid woodwork.

5. **uncanny** (un can′ nē)—A: amusing. B: mysterious. C: thoughtless. D: guileless.

6. **compendium** (com pen′ dē um)—A: summary. B: large desk. C: assurance. D: counterweight.

7. **ingestion** (in jes′ chun)—A: pain or discomfort. B: overcrowded state. C: eating. D: arrival.

8. **foible** (foy′ b'l)—A: artifice. B: personal fault. C: attitude. D: witticism.

9. **decade** (dĕk′ ād)—A: disintegration. B: trice. C: rhythmic tone. D: group of ten.

10. **poignant** (poin′ yant)—A: deeply moving. B: witty. C: obscure. D: savory.

11. **nebulous** (nĕb′ ū lus)—A: indefinite. B: voracious. C: opaque. D: indifferent.

12. **component** (com pō′ nent)—A: part. B: arrangement. C: niche. D: combination.

13. **nubby** (nub′ ē)—A: affectionate. B: chic. C: childlike. D: lumpy.

14. **tort**—A: remark. B: harmful act. C: legal form. D: gesture.

15. **effervescent** (ef ur ves′ ′nt)—A: alluring. B: bubbling. C: laundering. D: crystal-clear.

16. **caption** (cap′ shun)—A: joke. B: definition. C: title. D: problem.

17. **prone** (prōn)—A: rigid. B: persistent. C: predisposed. D: protective.

18. **finite** (fī′ nīt)—A: crucial. B: limited. C: precise. D: everlasting.

19. **occlusive** (ŏ klōō′ sĭv)—that which A: discriminates. B: outrages. C: distinguishes. D: shuts off.

20. **contend** (con tend′)—A: assert. B: approve. C: quibble. D: contradict.

ANSWERS

1. **invert**—C: To turn upside down or inside out; reverse. "*Invert* the cake onto a serving dish." Latin *invertere* (to turn over, transpose).

2. **redemption**—D: Buying back; exchanging coupons or stamps for a premium or prize. Latin *redemptio*.

3. **console**—C: Radio, phonograph or TV cabinet designed to stand on the floor. French.

4. **parquetry**—D: Inlaid woodwork forming a pattern, often of contrasting woods; as, a simulated *parquetry* top. French *parquet* (little park; small enclosure).

5. **uncanny**—B: Mysterious; eerie; as, the *uncanny* predictions of a seer. Scottish.

6. **compendium**—A: Short, comprehensive summary. Latin *compendere* (to weigh together); as, a *compendium* of useful information.

7. **ingestion**—C: Eating; the taking in of anything; as, the *ingestion* of vitamins. Latin *ingerere* (to carry; pour in).

8. **foible**—B: A slight, easily excusable personal fault or idiosyncrasy; as, our follies and *foibles*. Originally a fencing term, referring to the weak part of a sword. French.

9. **decade**—D: Group of ten; period of ten years. Greek *deka* (ten).

10. **poignant**—A: From Latin *pungere* (to prick); thus, emotionally moving in a painful, penetrating way; as, *poignant* memories.

11. **nebulous**—A: From the Latin *nebula* (cloud, mist). Indefinite; vague; unclear. "The problem of insecurity is *nebulous*."

12. **component**—A: A main part of a whole; as, top-quality, factory-tested *components*. Latin *componere* (to put together).

13. **nubby**—D: Lumpy; having a rough, knotted surface. Related to *nub* (knob, lump) from Middle Low German *knobbe* (knob). "Start with *nubby* textured drapery."

14. **tort**—B: Harmful act (such as injuring property or a reputation) for which a civil suit can be brought. "Such time lags are an indictment of the present *tort* system." Latin *torquere* (to twist).

15. **effervescent**—B: Bubbling up; foaming; as, unsurpassed *effervescent* action. Also lively; sparkling. Latin *effervescere* (to boil up).

16. **caption**—C: Title; short description of a picture in a publication; as, *captions* that are stories in themselves. Latin *capere* (to take, seize).

17. **prone**—C: Predisposed; as, students in their cavity-*prone* years. Latin *pronus* (inclined forward).

18. **finite**—B: Limited; having certain boundaries; as, the world's *finite* petroleum reserves. Latin *finire* (to finish).

19. **occlusive**—D: Shutting off; obstructing; as, "It sets up an *occlusive* seal." Latin *occludere*.

20. **contend**—A: To assert; maintain. Latin *contendere* (to strain, exert).

VOCABULARY RATINGS

20—19 correct ....exceptional
18—15 correct ....excellent
14—12 correct .... good

Don't Give Up
on English

BY WILL STANTON

The English language is like a woman's wardrobe—full of things she can't use, and yet the one thing she needs she can't find.

For instance, we don't have a good general interrogative like the French *N'est-ce pas?* One possibility is the word *Right?* The trouble is, people who start using it can't stop. "So, I'm driving down the street, right? And there's this big truck, right? Now, I'm not going to hassle any truck, right?"

And how do you contract *Am I not?* Amn't I? Ain't I? Aren't I? I can't use any one of these without feeling like a simpleton, so I'm forced back to *Am I not*. Right?

Then there are words which have been kicking around the language for centuries without ever doing a lick of honest work. Take *adumbrate,* which means to foreshadow or reveal, to overshadow or conceal, to outline in a shadowy way—or to reveal some, conceal some. It's like a dispenser that puts out salt, pepper, napkins and maple syrup all at once.

There are combinations of words that don't make sense. *Raise* means to build up; *raze* means to tear down—as, for instance, by burning up. Which means burning down.

Fasten is the opposite of *loosen*. But *unfasten* and *unloosen* are the same. If you *look over* something, you give it a good look. If you *overlook* it, you don't look at it at all. If you *oversee* it, you give it a good look again.

Then there's the way we put words together. You hear a cuddlesome girl referred to as *honey lamb*—as if a young sheep dipped in honey was something you might like to hug.

When a person does something stupid, we call him a *dumb bunny*. Like if he gets out of a warm bed to go outside in the wet bushes and hide Easter eggs. True, it's the bunny who gets credit for this idiocy, but who actually does it? And what do you suppose the bunny is doing meantime? Okay.

The English language is constantly changing, and it's not the experts who change it. It's the dummies who don't know any better.

The word *awful* used to mean something awe-inspiring like a cathedral. When a new church was built, everybody would go to see how *awful* it was. Sunday after Sunday. The kids would maybe rather have fooled around down at the creek or over at some girl's house. But no, back to the old cathedral. "You ever see such an awful church?" they'd say. "No, I've seen churches, but this takes the cake for awful." And they would cross their eyes and make gagging sounds, and the word acquired the meaning it has now.

According to the rules, you shouldn't end a sentence with a preposition. This is a rule I don't believe in. A preposition at the end gives a sentence zing—shows where it's at. My son seems to share the feeling. One time I went up to his room to read him a bedtime story and took the wrong book. He said, "What did you bring that book I didn't want to be read to out of up for?"

English has a rule that says two negatives make a positive. This may be all right for math, but it's a little unrealistic in practice. Let's say you ask a girl for a date and she says, "I don't want nothing to do with you, no time, no way." To an English professor she means yes. This may be one reason so many scholars wind up overcautious.

Two words that cause a lot of trouble are *lie* and *lay*. You can *lay* your head down or *lay* yourself down, but you can't just *lay down*. Unless it's the past tense. If you *lay down* half a second ago, that's fine. But right now you're not *laying*, you're *lying*. When the change takes place I don't know—and try explaining it to somebody from Albania.

Sit down and *set* are just as bad. A *setting* hen *sits* on the eggs. When she's *laying*, she's not *lying*—she's *sitting* again. The only time a chicken *lies down* is when it's dead. Just looking at a chicken, you'd never guess it led such a complicated life.

Don't get me wrong. I have no patience with people who say English is a "dying" language. That's not the word to describe it at all. The words you might use to describe English are the same ones you might apply to your wife: charming, exasperating, enchanting, maddening, unreasonable, beloved.

Beware These Word-Traps!

BY THEODORE M. BERNSTEIN

*Can you spot the misused word in the following sentence?
"It gentles the smoke by traveling it farther." Maybe this
one will help you: "We can sleep 20 people in the house
in a pinch, but we can eat only 12." For many years Theodore M. Bernstein, assistant managing editor of the* New
York Times, *campaigned against such misuse of our language. Here are extracts from his book,* The Careful Writer.

A.D. *Anno Domini* means in the year of our Lord, and
its abbreviation should not, therefore, be affixed to the name
of a century. "The sixth century A.D." would mean the
sixth century in the year of our Lord, which is preposterous.
Write "the sixth century after Christ" or, better still, just
"the sixth century."

ADAGE. "The press secretary recalled the old adage—
'vote early and often.'" An "adage" is a long-established
saying; therefore the "old" is redundant.

ARBITRATE, MEDIATE. They are not interchange-
able. "Arbitrators" hear evidence, act as judges. "Media-
tors" act as go-betweens to work out an agreement, but lack
the authority of ultimate decision.

ATTORNEY, LAWYER. "Lawyer" designates one who practices law. "Attorney" refers to one who is designated by another to transact business for him. An attorney may or may not be a lawyer, but a lawyer is an attorney only when he has a client. It may be that the desire of lawyers to appear to be making a go of their profession has accounted for their leaning toward the designation "attorney."

AVERT, AVOID. "The second war was different," said a British prime minister. "I don't think anything could have avoided it." Not true. Switzerland "avoided" it (*i.e.,* kept clear of it, shunned it). The prime minister meant that he did not think anything could have "averted" it (*i.e.,* prevented it, warded it off).

BLATANT, FLAGRANT. In "blatant" the emphasis is on noise; "blatant" means obnoxiously loud. "Flagrant" means openly evil or scandalous.

CAREEN, CAREER. "Careen" means to tilt or heel over: "The yacht careened sharply at the first buoy." "Career" means to move at high speed: "Out of control, the car careered into the children."

FLAIL, FLAY. "Who is to stay that ham-like hand when it flays away?" "Flay" means to tear the skin off. "Flail" means to whip or flog.

FLAMMABLE. Identical in meaning with *inflammable,* the variant "flammable" has for some years been pushed forward by fire underwriters. They argue—and no doubt with justice—that many people, on picking up a can of cleaning fluid labeled *inflammable,* believe the fluid will not burn. If it will save a single burned eyelash, by all means let's have "flammable."

GAMBIT. In chess, the word refers to opening moves in which a piece is sacrificed to obtain a strategic advantage. Derivatively, it means a concession to get things started. It does not mean *any* opening move, or merely a maneuver in the course of a game. If a lad wooing a lass invites her to dinner, it is not a "gambit"; if he in addition invests his hard-earned pay in orchids and champagne in the hope of a later return, it is.

GENDER. "Gender" is a grammatical term. It is not a substitute for "sex" (but, then, what is?).

KNOT. "The carrier *Wasp* is limping home at eight knots an hour." "Knot" is a unit of speed: one nautical mile an hour. Therefore "an hour" should never follow "knots."

MECCA. "The Yiddish Art Theater, which was a Mecca for Jewish theatergoers on New York's Lower East Side . . ." For Jews a Mecca yet! Which proves that a cliché can be explosive in the hands of the unwary.

NEAR-RECORD. "New York City registration, which ended last night, set a near-record." This is like saying, "The team scored three near-touchdowns." A similar example is this headline: "Near-Riot Is Averted at Hudson." What actually took place was, perhaps, a near-riot; what was averted was a full-fledged riot.

NON SEQUITURS. Irrelevancies often result from a writer's desire to work in a piece of information and his incapacity to determine where it should go. "Born in Des Moines, Mr. Tuttle joined Philip Ruxton in the business of making printing ink." No wonder a reader wrote to the newspaper: "Born in Waukegan, Ill., I get damn sick of *non sequiturs*."

PROPORTIONS. "A building of huge proportions." "Proportions" expresses a relationship of one part to another, or of parts to the whole. It has nothing to do with size. A better word would be "dimensions" or "size."

SELF-DEPRECATING. One can "depreciate" (belittle) oneself, but cannot normally "deprecate" (protest against, disapprove of) oneself.

SELF-MADE. A "self-made" man is a man who has made himself. But "The bulk of Mr. Getty's fortune is self-made"? Maybe that's what is meant by "an independent income."

STRANGLED. "He was found strangled to death." Delete "to death." That's what "strangled" means.

ZOOM. Originally an aviation term, "zoom" denotes rapid *upward* motion. The following sentence is therefore incorrect: "Melville zoomed down the incline." The writer may have had in mind the word "swoop." "Swoop" is usually down.

Word Power Test No. 11

Moderately Difficult Words

BY PETER FUNK

This collection of moderately difficult words will confirm the belief that the multi-syllable Greek and Latin words borrowed by English vastly enrich our tongue. But they also present barriers to students, spellers and test-takers. In the list below, most of which are from classic languages, check the word or phrase that you think is *nearest in meaning* to the key word. Answers appear at the end of this test.

1. **categorical** (kat ĕ gor′ ĭ kal)—A: orderly. B: absolute. C: stubborn. D: authoritative.

2. **proviso** (pro vī′ zo)—A: sanction. B: directive. C: stipulation. D: substitute.

3. **constraint** (kon strānt′)—A: restraint. B: compactness. C: intensity. D: aloofness.

4. **genial** (jēn′ yal)—A: spontaneous. B: easygoing. C: ingratiating. D: affable.

5. **accost** (ă kost′)—A: to charge. B: address. C: equip. D: ambush.

6. **unorthodox** (un or′ thō doks)—A: false. B: unsuitable. C: relaxed. D: not conventional.

7. **inalienable** (in āl′ yen a b′l)—A: unassailable. B: conflicting. C: irrevocable. D: irreconcilable.

8. **reappraisal** (re a prā′ zal)—A: revaluation. B: concise summary. C: survey. D: retaliatory act.

9. **savor** (sā′ ver)—A: to encourage. B: anticipate. C: relish. D: try.

10. **credulous** (kred′ ū lus)—A: skeptical. B: rash. C: honest. D: naïve.

11. **repetitive** (re pĕt′ ĭ tiv)—A: boring. B: persistent. C: repeating. D: irritating.

115

12. **ruminate** (rōō′ mǐ nāt)—A: to reflect. B: wander. C: talk at random. D: reside in the country.

13. **rescind** (rĕ sind′)—A: to admit error. B: retreat from a position. C: apologize and make amends. D: repeal or abrogate.

14. **advocate** (ad′ vo kāt)—A: to demand. B: agree to. C: continue. D: recommend.

15. **maverick** (mav′ er ik)—A: dissenter. B: miscreant. C: wild animal. D: deserter.

16. **protocol** (prō′ tō kŏl)—A: statecraft. B: formal ceremony. C: code of etiquette. D: official record.

17. **interrogate** (in ter′ o gāt)—A: to frighten. B: detain. C: bury. D: question.

18. **circuitous** (sir kū′ ĭ tus)—A: rounded. B: indirect. C: confusing. D: crooked.

19. **lesion** (lē′ zhun)—A: injury. B: fastening. C: throng. D: division.

20. **belittle** (be lit′ ′l)—A: to badger. B: disparage. C: mock. D: demote.

ANSWERS

1. **categorical**—B: Absolute; unqualified; without reservation; as, a *categorical* statement. Greek *katēgoria* (affirmation).

2. **proviso**—C: Stipulation; clause in a contract stating a condition or requirement; as, to add a cancellation *proviso*. Latin *proviso quod* (provided that).

3. **constraint**—A: Restraint; repression of one's true feelings; as, to debate the issue with *constraint*. Latin *constringere* (to constrict).

4. **genial**—D: Affable; kindly; cheerful; as, a *genial* host. Latin *genialis*.

5. **accost**—B: To address; approach and speak to; speak first to; as, to *accost* a stranger. Middle French *accoster*.

6. **unorthodox**—D: Not conventional; breaking with tradition; as, *unorthodox* dress. Greek *an-* (not), and *orthodoxos* (having a right opinion).

7. **inalienable**—C: Irrevocable; that cannot be taken away, transferred or surrendered; as, *inalienable* rights. French *inaliénable*.

8. **reappraisal**—A: Revaluation; new or fresh appraisal; as,

a *reappraisal* of one's objectives. Middle French *re-* (again) and *aprisier* (to set a value on).

9. **savor**—C: To relish; taste or enjoy thoroughly; as, to *savor* success. Latin *sapere* (to taste).

10. **credulous**—D: Naïve; overready to believe or trust; as, a *credulous* audience. Latin *credulus*, from *credere* (to believe).

11. **repetitive**—C: Repeating; marked by needless repetition; as, *repetitive* writing. Latin *repetere* (to repeat).

12. **ruminate**—A: To reflect; ponder at length; as, to *ruminate* on past errors. Latin *ruminare* (to chew over again).

13. **rescind**—D: To repeal or abrogate; make void. Latin *rescindere* (to cut away).

14. **advocate**—D: To recommend publicly; plead in favor of; support; as, to *advocate* a nationwide anti-pollution program. Latin *advocare* (to summon).

15. **maverick**—A: Dissenter; nonconforming individualist; as, a political *maverick*. After Samuel A. *Maverick*, a Texas pioneer who did not brand his cattle.

16. **protocol**—C: Code of diplomatic etiquette and precedence; as, to be seated according to *protocol*. Greek *prōtokollon*.

17. **interrogate**—D: To question formally and systematically; as, to *interrogate* a prisoner. Latin *interrogare*.

18. **circuitous**—B: Indirect; roundabout; as, a *circuitous* route. Latin *circuitus*, from *circumire* (to go round).

19. **lesion**—A: Injury; impairment; damage to the body; as, a *lesion* in a tendon. Latin *laedere* (to injure).

20. **belittle**—B: To disparage; decry; speak slightingly of; as, to *belittle* an opponent's record.

VOCABULARY RATINGS

20—18 correct ....excellent
17—15 correct .... good
14—12 correct .... fair

A Tip on Straight Thinking

BY STUART CHASE

In an English law court the attorney for the defense was handed a note by his partner: "No case. Abuse the plaintiff's attorney." The defendant was guilty on the evidence, so the best his attorney could do was to try to confuse the jury by making a reprehensible character out of the lawyer on the other side.

This type of argument has been around a long time—so long indeed that it has a Latin name, *argumentum ad hominem*. This means to switch the argument from the issue to the man, and might be freely translated, "Get personal." If a case is hard to attack on its merits, attack the character of the man in charge.

The power to reason accurately has been called the chief glory of man. Every day, almost every hour, by an astonishing process inside the brain, we form opinions and make decisions. Our conclusions can be good, bad or indifferent, depending on how we have learned to think.

Wise men over the centuries have identified about 20

varieties of false and phony reasoning. Argument *ad hominem* easily heads the list.

About a century ago Darwin and Huxley evolved the principles of evolution. Many religious people were shocked and tremendous opposition developed. Bishop Wilberforce was especially shocked, and in a public debate asked Huxley: "Are you descended from a monkey on your grandmother's or your grandfather's side?" This classic example of *ad hominem* brought down the house. Rather than debate the scientific evidence, the Bishop evaded the issue by resorting to a crack about Huxley's ancestors.

Some years ago I was asked to testify in a legal action in Bridgeport, Conn. I had been working on population trends in the United States, and a committee wanted me to apply the formulas to forecast the growth of Bridgeport. The case had to do with a new city reservoir. The lawyer for the other side began by questioning my figures. This was right and proper. Finding no serious discrepancies, he shuffled his notes, took a step in my direction and demanded, "Mr. Chase, were you ever a Technocrat?"

What this had to do with the population prospects of Bridgeport was a trifle obscure; but it was intended to discredit me as a witness. Technocrats were supposed to be crackpots. I said I'd never been a Technocrat. At the peak of the Technocracy craze, I went on, I had written an article about it. Thus I managed to meet this *ad hominem* squeeze play, but plenty of other witnesses do not.

There are all sorts of *ad hominem* cases. We all have heard the complaint that Smith's plan for traffic control in our town can't be any good because Smith never went beyond grade school. This conclusion saves us the trouble of studying the plan. We all know the father who laughs off Junior's idea as to why the family car coughs like a wounded gorilla. The notion must be worthless, Father thinks, because Junior is still so very junior. But he may have a passion for internal-combustion engines.

There is another Latin term which links up here: *non sequitur*, "it does not follow." Because a man has his faults it does not follow that what he has produced, sponsored or is associated with is worthless. By the same token, because the man is beyond praise, it does not follow that his every idea is too good to be looked into.

Ad hominem, once grasped, alerts us to many pitfalls in thinking. Presently we can spot it snarling up television and radio discussion programs, news stories, editorials, political speeches—especially political speeches. We find it reappearing in the arguments of our family and our friends. But let me warn you not to be overzealous in correcting family and friends. Start slowly, as in a golf swing. Nobody likes to be told he doesn't know how to think. What one of us, however, isn't glad to be able to think a little straighter?

To avoid faulty, unfair and sometimes disastrous decisions, squeeze the personality out of an issue. Stop and ask: "Is the idea sound, regardless of its origin? Am I judging the matter on its merits, or am I getting personal?"

Masters
of Babble

BY JAMES P. DEGNAN

The scene is my office. I am at work, doing what must be done to help cure a disease that, over the years, I have come to call straight-A illiteracy. I am interrogating, I am cross-examining, I am prying and probing for the meaning of a student's paper. The student is a college senior with a straight-A average, an extremely bright student who has just been awarded a coveted fellowship for postgraduate study. He and I have been at this for an hour.

"The choice of exogenous variables in relation to mul-ticolinearity," I hear myself reading from his paper, "is contingent upon the derivations of certain multiple corre-lation coefficients." I pause to catch my breath. "Now that statement," I address the student—whom I shall call, al-legorically, Mr. Bright—"that statement, Mr. Bright—what on earth does it mean?"

Mr. Bright, brow furrowed, tries mightily. Finally, com-bining our mental resources, we decode it. We discover what he is trying to say, what he really *wants* to say, which is: "Supply determines demand."

Over the past decade or so, I have known many college seniors suffering from "Bright's disease." It attacks the best minds, and gradually destroys the critical faculties. During the years of higher education, it grows worse, reaching its terminal stage, typically, when its victim receives his Ph.D. Obviously, the victim is no ordinary illiterate. He would never turn in a paper with misspellings or errors in punctuation; he would never use a double negative or the word *irregardless*. Nevertheless, he *is* illiterate, in the worst way. He is incapable of saying, in writing, simply and clearly, what he means.

The ordinary illiterate might say: "Them people down at the shop better stock up on what our customers need, or we ain't gonna be in business long." Not our man. Taking his cue from years of higher education, years of reading the textbooks and professional journals that are the major sources of his affliction, he writes: "The focus of concentration must rest upon objectives centered around the knowledge of customer areas so that a sophisticated awareness of those areas can serve as an entrepreneurial filter to screen what is relevant from what is irrelevant to future commitments." For writing such gibberish he is awarded A's on his papers and the opportunity to move, inexorably, toward his Ph.D.

The major cause of such illiteracy is the stuff the straight-A illiterate is forced to read during his years of higher education. He learns to write gibberish by reading it, and by being taught to admire it. He must grapple with such journals as the *American Sociological Review*, journals bulging with barbarous jargon, such as "ego-integrative action orientation." In such journals, two things are never described as being "alike." They are "homologous" or "isomorphic." Nor are things simply "different." They are "allotropic." In such journals, writers never "divide" anything. They "dichotomize" or "bifurcate."

Sociology has long been notorious for producing illiterates of all kinds, but such supposedly more literate and humane disciplines as philosophy, and even English, turn them out as well. If the potential victim majors in English with an emphasis on linguistics, it will be almost impossible for him to emerge with literacy intact. He will habitually read such masters of babble as Dr. Noam Chomsky or Dr. Zellig S. Harris. From Chomsky's *Syntactic Structures:* "When transformational analysis is properly formulated we find that it is essentially more powerful than description in terms of phrase structure, just as the latter is essentially more powerful than description in terms of finite-state Markov processes that generate sentences from left to right." Or from Dr. Harris's renowned text, *Structural Linguistics:* "Another consideration is the availability of simultaneity, in addition to successivity, as a relation among linguistic elements."

Such reading reduces the student's mind to gruel. His capacity to think degenerates, and, with it, his capacity to write readable English.

From time to time, visionaries and radicals have tried to do away with straight-A illiteracy but, obviously, to little effect. Yet the cure is simple. The various academic disciplines need to recognize the homely truth that the one thing they share, and *must* share if they are to communicate with one another, is a common language—a language with conventions and standards that determine whether it is being used well or badly. These criteria are available in such civilized (but, these days, apparently unused) sources as Fowler's *Modern English Usage* and the standard dictionaries.

Writing well means writing simply, clearly, vividly and forcefully, whether such writing is done by a philosopher or an engineer. If one has nothing to say, one should refrain from using thousands of words to say it; pretentious nonsense is not profundity.

These truths are painful for many. As one of the many straight-A illiterates I have known once explained, "If I followed your advice, I could never write the 5000-word term papers I am regularly assigned; I could never get a fellowship to graduate school, or a contract to do a textbook, or a decent job in business or government. What you're asking is just too much. Think what it would do in the universities alone. It would wipe out hundreds of courses and all of the colleges of education. And think what it would do to the economy; think of the depression it would cause in the paper and ink and business-machine industries; think what would happen in the publishing business; think of all the secretaries who would be out of work. No, I'm sorry, literacy might be okay, but I can't afford it."

Word Power Test No. 12

Book Words

BY PETER FUNK

This collection of words comes from books, and shows it. There is something lofty and impressive about "book words". They seem to go about in formal attire, unlike the shirt-sleeves words of everyday talk. In the list below, check the word or phrase that you think is nearest in meaning to the key word. Answers appear at the end of this test.

1. **accede** (ak sēd')—A: to reach. B: achieve. C: assent. D: go beyond.

2. **proponent** (pro pō' nent)—A: adversary. B: interpreter. C: dissenter. D: advocate.

3. **gradation** (gra dā' shun)—A: gradual change. B: placement. C: evaluation. D: measuring mark.

4. **interstice** (in ter' stis)—A: legal ban. B: narrow space. C: dividing line. D: insert.

5. **reproof** (re prōōf')—A: rebuke. B: warning. C: lampoon. D: duplicate.

6. **paean** (pē' an)—A: peasant. B: offering. C: song of praise. D: heathen.

7. **countermand** (koun ter mand')—A: to strengthen. B: prohibit. C: smuggle. D: revoke.

8. **blazon** (blā' zun)—A: to publicize. B: burn. C: smooth. D: mark.

9. **expiate** (eks' pǐ āt)—A: to speed up. B: atone for. C: make clear. D: forgive.

10. **concentric** (kon sen' trik)—A: round. B: condensed. C: having a common center. D: simultaneous.

11. **verity** (ver' ǐ tē)—A: conceit. B: assortment. C: guarantee. D: truth.

12. **modulate** (mod' ū lāt)—A: to update. B: regulate. C: intervene. D: compromise.

13. **cupidity** (kū pid′ ĭ tē)—A: stinginess. B: infatuation. C: curiosity. *D*: greed.

14. **adventitious** (ad ven tish′ us)—A: helpful. B: favorable. C: accidental. *D*: timely.

15. **pastoral** (pas′ tor al)—*A*: rural. B: sentimental. C: historic. D: isolated.

16. **on tenterhooks** (ten′ ter hooks)—A: detained. *B*: cautious. C: anxious. D: having resilience.

17. **kinetic** (kĭ net′ ik)—A: collective. *B*: pertaining to motion. C: psychic. D: related by blood.

18. **transfix** (trans fiks′)—A: to close up. B: substitute. *C*: impale. D: redo.

19. **descry** (de skrī′)—A: to catch sight of. B: describe. *C*: complain. D: belittle.

20. **caprice** (ka prēs′)—A: illusion. B: whim. *C*: grace. D: practical joke.

ANSWERS

1. **accede**—C: To assent; consent; yield, often under pressure; as, to *accede* to terms of a peace settlement. Latin *accedere* (to approach).

2. **proponent**—D: Advocate; one who makes a proposal; as, the *proponent* of a broad conservation program. Latin *proponere* (to put forth).

3. **gradation**—A: Gradual change by regular degrees or stages; as, the distinct *gradations* of the solar spectrum. Latin *gradus* (step).

4. **interstice**—B: Narrow space between things or parts; chink; crevice; as, the moss-filled *interstices* of the old wall. Latin *intersistere* (to stand between).

5. **reproof**—A: Rebuke; expression of mild disapproval; as, conduct warranting parental *reproof*. Old French *reprover* (to reprove).

6. **paean**—C: Song of joyful praise or triumph; as, a *paean* to freedom. Latin *paean*.

7. **countermand**—D: To revoke or reverse, as a command; cancel; as, to *countermand* an order for merchandise. Middle French *contremander*.

8. **blazon**—A: To publicize widely; exhibit conspicuously; also, to deck; adorn; as, to *blazon* the town with posters. Middle French *blason*.

9. **expiate**—B: To atone for; make amends for; as, to *expiate* an offense. Latin *expiare*.

10. **concentric**—C: Having a common center, as circles within one another; as, *concentric* circles on the water. Latin *com-* (together) and *centrum* (center).

11. **verity**—D: Truth; true statement; accurate fact; as, to challenge the *verity* of a witness's testimony. Latin *verus* (true).

12. **modulate**—B: To regulate; soften; tone down; adjust to an appropriate quality or volume; as, to *modulate* one's voice. Latin *modulari* (to measure).

13. **cupidity**—D: Greed; avarice; inordinate desire for wealth or possessions; as, the *cupidity* of irresponsible pre-emptors of our natural resources. Latin *cupere* (to desire).

14. **adventitious**—C: Accidental; occurring unexpectedly or in other than the usual location; as an *adventitious* weed. Latin *adventicius* (coming from the outside).

15. **pastoral**—A: Rural; having the simplicity and charm of country life; as, a quiet, *pastoral* scene. Latin *pastor* (herdsman).

16. **on tenterhooks**—C: Anxious; a state of suspense, as though "stretched." Latin *tendere* (to stretch) and Old English *hoc* (hook). A *tenterhook* is a hook for fastening cloth on a tenter, a stretching frame.

17. **kinetic**—B: Pertaining to motion and the forces associated with motion; lively; as, the *kinetic* excitement of ice hockey. Greek *kinein* (to move).

18. **transfix**—C: To impale; pierce through; immobilize as if by piercing; as, to be *transfixed* with horror. Latin *transfigere*.

19. **descry**—A: To catch sight of; discern by careful scanning something distant and difficult to view; as, to *descry* the misty mountain peak. Old French *descrier*.

20. **caprice**—B: Whim; impulsive or unpredictable change without apparent reason; as, the *caprice* of the weather. Italian *capriccio*.

VOCABULARY RATINGS

20—18 correct ....exceptional
17—15 correct ....excellent
14—12 correct .... good

There's a Meaning Here Somewhere

BY EDWIN NEWMAN

The day is not far off when someone about to join his family will excuse himself by saying that he does not want to keep his micro-cluster of structured role expectations waiting.

True, I came upon this gem of social-scientific jargon in London, but that only shows how far our influence has spread and how determined the British are to join the Americans at the kill when the English language finally is done to death. Asphyxiation will be the cause, with the lethal agent gas. This is the gas which, added to evidence, produces evidentiary material, and which, escaping from a Secret Service spokesman, turned former President Ford and *his* micro-cluster of structured role expectations into protectees. At that, protectee is better than a similar government word, escapee, which is used—misused—to mean somebody who escaped.

"To what do you attribute your escape?"

"I am a fast runnee."

The chief current protectee of the Secret Service is not

a gross offender—or offendee—against the language, though he once identified inflation as "the universal enemy of one hundred percent of our people." Alan Greenspan, chairman of the Council of Economic Advisers, had a bit more to say about the same subject: "Thus, once the inflation genie has been let out of the bottle, it is a very tricky policy problem to find the particular calibration and timing that would be appropriate to stem the acceleration in risk premiums created by falling incomes without prematurely aborting the decline in the inflation-generated risk premiums. This is clearly not an easy policy path to traverse, but it is the path which we must follow."

Greenspan was speaking in Washington, a city where a scarcity of money is routinely referred to as a tight resource environment and where, after an experiment with fish in which all the fish died, the Atomic Energy Commission said, "The biota exhibited one-hundred-percent mortality response."

Thrust is also a word much in vogue today. A dean of a university department of home economics (no longer called home economics but family resources and consumer sciences) told an interviewer that in her previous job, in the Office of Education in Washington, most of her work had been in "conceptualizing new thrusts in programming."

Conceptualizing thrusts, or articulating them, is what we have come to expect from the social sciences. In that world, a sociologist will feel that he has advanced the cause of knowledge by classifying murder and assault as escalated interpersonal altercations; an applicant for a grant for technical training will write, "A quality void in technical capacity constrains achievement"; and teachers who encourage children will be said to emit reinforcers. It was a social scientist who wrote that knowledge that is transmitted from person to person *qua* knowledge is called intersubjectively transmissible knowledge or, for the sake of brevity, transmissible knowledge. Making knowledge something of a bridge over the river *qua*.

I do not wish to overlook the contribution of business to wrecking the language. B. Altman, in New York, has issued this invitation: "Sparkle your table with Cape Cod classic glassware." As it happened, I did not have time to sparkle my table because I was busy following instructions given in another advertisement and was accessorizing my spacious master bedroom with oil paintings and, in the words of another advertisement that appeared in *The New Yorker*, "making beautiful happen to [my] window treatments . . ." Some days, I wish I could just make *clean* happen to my window treatments.

When it comes to making language mushy and boneless, the British are perhaps not quite as resourceful as the Americans. For instance, playwright William Douglas-Home, writing to *The Times* of London, said that the Conservative Party "should be plugging, day in, day out, the true facts about taxation." True facts are, of course, the only kind of facts available—but see what a press release for an American television program does with them: "The facts hew to actuality." True facts. The facts hew to actuality. No contest.

But don't cheer, folks. Soon, also, no language.

The Most Nerve-Shattering Word in the Language

BY H. ALLEN SMITH

Lullaby. Golden. Damask. Moonlight. Do these words seem esthetically attractive to you? They have appeared with some regularity on lists of "the ten most beautiful words in our language." Along with luminous, and hush, anemone, mother and various others. These lists appear from time to time in the public prints. But I can't recall ever seeing a list of the ten ugliest words in the language.

Almost every literate person has in his head an agglomeration of words that can cause him to wince, and even shudder, such as agglomeration. I lay claim to several hundred of the uglies. Mulcted almost nauseates me. I cringe in the face of albeit, and/or, yclept, obsequies, whilom, and tinsmith. Want to hear a *real* ugly word? Ugly.

But my own nomination for the meanest and low-down-est and ugliest word of them all is "Oh." Said twice, with maybe a hyphen, this way: "Oh-oh." In its maximal ugliness, it is customarily spoken softly with inflections that would curl the toes of a sandy-land mule.

Something is wrong, let us say, with the engine of your car. You take it to the garage. The mechanic lifts the hood and pokes around a bit and then you hear him murmur, "Oh-oh." The wretched creature says it in such a quietly dramatic manner that you know instantly that your whole motor has to be derricked out and thrown away and a new one put in.

Consider our friends, the dentists. Most of them have enough gumption (beautiful word!) to conceal their opinions and judgments, but sometimes you'll run across one who forgets his chairside manner. He'll be inspecting a big molar in the back, and suddenly he'll say, "Oh-oh." Or he'll come out of his darkroom carrying an X ray taken a few minutes earlier, and he'll put it up against the light, and he'll look at it briefly, and then his head will give a jerk and he'll say, "Oh-oh." You know at once, without ESP, precisely what is meant. Out. All of them. From now on, plates. No apples. No corn on the cob. No a lot of things.

Physicians as a general thing have schooled themselves carefully to conceal any sinister condition they may find during an examination. Yet I have run across one offender in my checkered medical career. He was giving me the annual checkup. He took my blood pressure and tapped me for knee jerks and scratched me on the bottoms of my feet for God knows what and stethoscoped me front and back and had me blow into a machine to test my "vital capacity" and then he turned the electrocardiograph loose on me. As he studied the saw-toothed dossier on my heart, his brow crinkled and I heard him say, quite softly, "Oh-oh." Everything inside of me suddenly bunched together in one large knot.

"What is it?" I demanded. "Whad you find there?"

"It's nothing, really," he said.

Nothing! Cancer of the heart is *nothing?* It had to be at least that.

"I heard you say 'Oh-oh.'" I told him. "Come on. Tell me. I'm a man. I can take it. Let me have it straight."

"Okay," he said, and I steeled myself and began to turn chicken. "I said 'Oh-oh' because," he went on, "I just happened to think that I haven't made out my tax return yet, and the deadline is tomorrow."

I quit him the next day. I can't use a doctor who is mooning over his income-tax return while he is looking at the record of my frightful heart disorders. I don't want a doctor *ever* to say "Oh-oh" in my presence, unless perhaps he has dropped his sphygmomanometer on the floor and busted it. Even in that contingency I think he should employ a more masculine expression. I would.

"Oh-oh" is the most frightening, nerve-shattering locution to come into general usage since Noah Webster's day. It should surely be forbidden by federal statute.

IT PAYS TO ENRICH YOUR WORD POWER ®

Word Power Test No. 13

From the Writings of Margaret Mead

BY PETER FUNK

The late Margaret Mead, one of the world's foremost anthropologists, was keenly aware of the vital role language plays in a culture, and was herself a skilled writer and lecturer. She used the following words in her autobiography, *Blackberry Winter*. Pick the word or phrase you believe is *nearest in meaning* to the key word.

Check your results at the end of this test.

1. **juxtapose** (juk′ stă pōz)—to place A: beyond. B: opposite. C: side by side. D: above.

2. **antidote** (an′ tĭ dōt)—A: epithet. B: short story. C: remedy. D: a proceeding.

3. **sacrosanct** (săk′ rō sankt)—A: peaceful. B: sacred. C: mundane. D: painful.

4. **admonition** (ad mo nish′ un)—A: reproof. B: pardon. C: award. D: amazement.

5. **stymie** (stī′ mē)—A: to delay. B: shorten. C: handicap. D: block.

6. **ruse** (rōōz)—A: a taunt. B: illusion. C: shrewdness. D: trick.

7. **parody** (păr′ o dē)—A: ploy. B: comparison. C: imitation. D: repetition.

8. **differentiate** (diff uh ren′ shē āt)—A: to protest. B: note differences between. C: estrange. D: shift.

9. **premise** (prĕm′ is)—A: assumption. B: outline. C: commitment. D: irrefutable fact.

10. **replicate** (rĕp′ lĭ kāt)—A: to establish. B: demonstrate. C: substitute. D: duplicate.

11. **impertinent** (im pur′ ti nent)—A: irritable. B: thoughtless. C: skeptical. D: impudent.

12. **contrapuntal** (con tra pun′ t′l)—A: aggressive. B: presenting contrasting elements. C: showing poor sense. D: eccentric.

13. **discern** (dĭ surn′)—A: to perceive. B: scatter. C: scrutinize. D: put together.

14. **precursor** (prē kur′ sur)—A: pursuer. B: hunch. C: foe. D: forerunner.

15. **utilitarian** (ū til ĭ tair′ ē un)—A: heat-producing. B: unimaginative. C: comprehensive. D: practical.

16. **artifact** (ar′ tĭ fact)—an object that is A: natural. B: an exact copy. C: man-made. D: synthetic.

17. **prevision** (prē vizh′ un)—related to A: food supplies. B: ideals. C: foresight. D: idolatry.

18. **pander**—A: to comfort. B: cater to others′ weaknesses. C: take unlawfully. D: implore.

19. **stance**—A: culture. B: jungle hut. C: forest. D: posture.

20. **rife** (rīf)—A: prevalent. B: competitive. C: divided. D: sharp.

ANSWERS

1. **juxtapose**—C: To place side by side. From French. "Past and present were *juxtaposed*."

2. **antidote**—C: Remedy to counteract a poison or any unwanted condition; as, an *antidote* to a humdrum life. Greek *antidoton* from *anti-* (against) and *dotos* (given).

3. **sacrosanct**—B: Sacred; holy; inviolable. Latin *sacrosanctus*. "The dwelling was *sacrosanct*."

4. **admonition**—A: Friendly reproof; mild warning or reminder. Latin *admonere*.

5. **stymie**—D: In golf, to place a ball in the way of another ball on a putting green; figuratively, to block. Scottish origin. "Our plans were *stymied*."

6. **ruse**—D: Trick or stratagem intended to deceive. Old French *reuser* (to turn aside; detour so as to throw dogs off the scent).

7. **parody**—C: Any humorous or mocking imitation; as, his recourse to sarcasm and bitter *parody*. Greek *paroidia* (countersong).

8. **differentiate**—B: To note differences between similar elements. Latin *differentia* (difference).

9. **premise**—A: Assumption or belief on which an argument

or conclusion is based; as, to keep one's *premises* clear. Latin *praemittere* (to send on ahead).

10. **replicate**—D: To duplicate; copy; repeat. Latin *replicare* (to fold back; review).

11. **impertinent**—D: Impudent; rude; as, an *impertinent* reply. Latin *impertinens* from *in-* (not) and *pertinere* (to reach out).

12. **contrapuntal**—B: Presenting contrasting elements in music, stories, etc. Italian *contrappunto* (pointed against).

13. **discern**—A: To perceive mentally or visually; to make a distinction; as, to *discern* a pattern. Latin *discernere* (to distinguish).

14. **precursor**—D: A forerunner that indicates future events or paves the way for achievements of others; predecessor; as, the unconscious mind in man's *precursors*. Latin *praecurrere* (to run before).

15. **utilitarian**—D: Practical; pragmatic; as, a *utilitarian* relationship. Latin *utilis* (useful).

16. **artifact**—C: A man-made object such as a tool or weapon. Latin *ars* (skill) and *facere* (to do).

17. **prevision**—C: Foresight; foreknowledge; prophecy or prediction; as, his *prevision* of the electronic revolution. Latin *praevisus*, from *prae videre* (to foresee).

18. **pander**—B: To cater to or exploit the weaknesses or worst desires in others; as, to *pander* to their greed. From the mythical Greek *Pandaros*, characterized in medieval stories as a go-between in love affairs.

19. **stance**—D: Posture; way of standing. Figuratively, one's intellectual or emotional attitude; as, the *stance* of American Indians. Old French *estance* (position).

20. **rife**—A: Prevalent or widespread, suggesting a rapid increase of something undesirable. Old English *ryfe* (abundant).

VOCABULARY RATINGS

20—19 correct ....exceptional
18—15 correct ....excellent
14—12 correct ....(. good)

As Silly
as a Simile

BY JANE GOODSELL

As easy as *what?* As pie? Listen, it's hard work to make a good pie. Even a not-so-good one can take the better part of a morning, what with all that mixing and flouring and rolling and fitting and crimping, not to mention preparing the filling and cleaning up afterward. Easy as pie, my eye!

A memory like an elephant's? Elephants are just as forgetful as anybody else, the only difference being that a poor memory is no great handicap to them. What does an elephant have to remember?

As sure as shootin' . . . as funny as hell . . . as blind as a bat . . . who dreams up these expressions anyway? They're easy to use—because everyone understands what they mean, even though they don't mean anything. But, as Anatole France rightly pointed out, "If 50 million people say a foolish thing, it is still a foolish thing."

Yet, at their best, similes have a right-on-target sharpness that makes language come alive. By aptly comparing one thing to another, they create word pictures that flash on the mind in perfect focus: as fresh as the morning dew, as dry as dust, as bright as a new penny, as free as the breeze. These similes are deft, explicit and precise.

Then there are the similes that aren't quite top-drawer, but which hang together reasonably well, give or take a bit of slack:

AS QUICK AS A WINK. On condition that it's a quick wink and not the suggestive, slo-o-o-w as molasses type, currently in vogue.

AS WHITE AS A SHEET. This used to be a sensible simile, so maybe it's worth preserving for old times' sake. But if you've patronized a white sale lately, you've doubtless noticed that bed linen comes in every color of the rainbow—plus candy stripes and psychedelic prints.

AS PLAIN AS DAY. Whatever this means, it's too vague to argue about.

AS PRETTY AS A PICTURE. We-ell, maybe. Some pictures *are* pretty, paintings of one-eyed ladies and tomato-soup cans notwithstanding.

While not quite as sound as a dollar (a non-inflationary dollar, that is), these similes are more or less rational. But when a figure of speech makes no sense, it has no business being one. Like, for example:

AS EASY AS TAKING CANDY FROM A BABY. Easy for whom? Separating a baby from a lollipop requires the hardheartedness of the Marquis de Sade. Less steely candy-snatchers turn to jelly when subjected to the infant's anguished sobs and fist-beating fury.

AS WARM AS TOAST. Of all things to pick as an example of warmth! By the time a slice of toast has been transferred to a plate, spread with butter and maybe a bit of marmalade, "as cool as toast" would be more like it.

AS CUTE AS A BUG. This is a compliment? Judging from the vast quantities of insecticide purchased annually, there's a lot of anti-bug sentiment around. While I can't speak for everybody, I'd say the average person is less inclined to chuck a bug under the chin than to spray it. A bug who feels snug in a rug is living in a fool's paradise.

AS RIGHT AS RAIN. On rare occasions—when it comes after a four-month drought or in lieu of a predicted blizzard—rain is right as right can be. But under ordinary circumstances it's no cause for celebration. On the contrary, it infuriates golfers, irks birdwatchers, enrages baseball fans, agitates mothers-of-the-bride and vexes ordinary citizens who left their umbrellas at home.

AS BROWN AS A BERRY. Although I'm no horticultural expert, I'd say offhand that berries come in every color *but* brown. Is there such a thing as a brown berry? If this rare item exists (Where? On the upper slopes of Mt. Kilimanjaro?), it still seems a farfetched example to represent such a common, everyday color.

These similes are as wrong as rain at a garden wedding, and as hard as pie to forget even if you have a memory as short as an elephant's. Matter of fact, the whole simile situation is in apple-pie disorder, as anyone who isn't as dull as a button will agree.

I Know Whatcha Mean

BY CLIFTON FADIMAN

Dr. Ellsworth Barnard, while visiting lecturer at Bowdoin College, proposed that high schools throughout the country revamp their English courses to teach rules "that conform to actual usage." Dr. Barnard went on to say, "Anything is all right if it fits the occasion and expresses the intended thought." The *New York Times*, reporting this pronouncement from the college once attended by Hawthorne and Longfellow, headed the dispatch: PROF SAYS BUM ENGLISH AIN'T SO BAD AFTER ALL.

There seems little doubt that the Levelers, increasingly backed by the authority of the Learned, have won their war. Our language has been made safe for democracy. What would, let us say in Mr. Hoover's time, have been thought of as illiteracy has been promoted to the rank of homespun American. The Levelers' thesis is now generally accepted: as our tongue is at any point merely the product of an infinity of small folk-initiated changes, the nasty notion of "correctness" falls to the ground, and there, we may well say, it lays. Things get easier every day; we never had it so good.

The leaders of the Levelers are the mass-communicators, particularly in radio and television. Perhaps, bowing to the inevitable, it is time to make Televenglish retroactive: that is, to revise the English of the past much as the Stalinists revised the history of the Russian revolution. Just as the latter substituted Stalin for Trotsky, so ought we to substitute the Winstonian* "like" for the fascist-reactionary-imperialist "as." (Example: Like the hart panteth after the water brooks, so panteth my soul after thee.—King David) And perhaps it is best to bow, not rear the head (in fact, it is best not to use the head at all) when you hear Billy Graham's benediction: "And may the Lord bless you *real good*."

Do not feel bad when you hear the broadcaster say he feels badly. Just remember that all men are created equally. When the friendly emcee shyly confides to his millions of listeners that he feels nauseous, do not misinterpret this as self-criticism. Applaud the Televenglish teacher who reiterates that Ford Is America's Winningest Car, who describes gorilla warfare and who reports that so-and-so flew *into* Chicago today.

From here on we should accept with equanimity the Levelese law by which the originally jocular becomes the universally mandatory. Thus, always say *Longtime no see. How's about a drink? He's scared but good*. Those kind of people are high-type fellas, just like you and I, and you can say that again.

Some time ago, on a TV show dealing with words, I was properly taken to task by a distinguished professor of English because I objected to the rate at which sounds were being dropped from the language. He informed me that such snobbish purism had no basis in logic. To be consistent, for instance, I should pronounce *gossamer* as *goose summer*, of which the word is a contraction.

I accepted the rebuke, both to my scholarship and to my character. Hereafter I shall speak Televenglish. If I wish to be helpful I shall be kwopertive. Traveling by air will

---

*"Winston tastes good, *like* a cigarette should."

become flĩng; the state of being safe will become scurty (*u* as in cure). And, as more and more New Yorkers exchange the distasteful *you will* in favor of the elegant *yizzle* (yizzle have to see Radio City), I shall follow their lead.

One of my correspondents, Miss Esther L. Johnson, sends me a paragraph lifted from an editorial comment in an old *Youth's Companion*, dated March 1, 1923. It reads:

> There are several engaging thoughts as to what the outcome of the widespread use of radio will be. Not the least pleasing of them is the idea that thousands of boys and girls will listen for an hour or more a day to a fair sort of spoken English, clearly enunciated. Youth is quick and imitative. Let us hope that on the waves of the ether may come lessons that will enlarge our vocabulary and improve our pronunciation.

How pleasant for Miss Johnson and for us all that it has taken only 40 years for this pious hope to become a shining reality.

IT PAYS TO ENRICH YOUR WORD POWER®

Word Power
Test No. 14

Headliners—News in a Nutshell

BY PETER FUNK

A good headline is the ultimate condensation—giving you the essence of a news report at a glance. The key words in the following test have been taken from newspaper headlines. Check the word or phrase you believe is *nearest in meaning* to the key word. The correct answers appear at the end of this test.

1. **flex** (fleks)—A: to separate. B: flip. C: bend. D: relax.
2. **insurgent** (in sur′ jent)—A: rebel. B: eccentric. C: emigrant. D: spy.
3. **rift**—A: ridge. B: tide. C: turmoil. D: split.
4. **medley** (měd′ lē)—A: mediocrity. B: hodgepodge. C: mystery. D: smoothness.
5. **impropriety** (im prō prī′ ĕ tē)—A: improper conduct. B: candor. C: thoughtlessness. D: poverty.
6. **quandary** (kwon′ dă rē)—A: state of uncertainty. B: large constellation. C: rambling discourse. D: a measurement.
7. **purge** (purj)—A: to submerge. B: thrust. C: cleanse. D: swirl.
8. **bewail** (bē wāl′)—A: to scourge. B: besmirch. C: accuse. D: lament.
9. **renege** (rē nĭg′)—A: to snub. B: go back on your word. C: dominate. D: renegotiate.
10. **scrutinize** (skrōō′ tĭ nīz)—A: to scrub thoroughly. B: join tightly. C: examine carefully. D: ignore.
11. **relic** (rěl′ ĭk)—A: talisman. B: rarity. C: common item. D: historic object.
12. **perky** (per′ kē)—A: pretty. B: smart. C: spirited. D: humorous.
13. **defector** (dē fěk′ tor)—One who A: destroys. B: deserts. C: advocates. D: deprograms.

142

14. **plebeian** (plē bē′ an)—A: hermit. B: bigot. C: aristocrat. D: common man.

15. **monitor** (mŏn′ ĭ tor)—One who A: scolds. B: warns. C: maintains. D: patrols.

16. **composite** (kŏm pŏz′ it)—A: compound. B: fake. C: solid. D: helical.

17. **scenario** (sĕ nĕr′ ē ō)—A: lasso. B: panorama. C: diorama. D: synopsis of a play.

18. **beguile** (bē gīl′)—A: to confuse. B: envy. C: charm. D: paralyze.

19. **rivet** (rĭv′ it)—A: to fasten firmly. B: tear apart. C: be curious about. D: complete.

20. **remedial** (rē mē′ dē ul)—Pertaining to A: averaging. B: recycling. C: remedying. D: speeding.

ANSWERS

1. **flex**—C: Bend or tighten. Latin *flectere* (to bend). "Congress Will *Flex* Its Foreign Policy Muscle."

2. **insurgent**—A: Rebel; one who revolts against authority. Latin *insurgens* (rising up against). "Union *Insurgent* Put Down by Meany."

3. **rift**—D: Split; break in friendly relations. Of Scandinavian origin. "New Wealth Brings Marital *Rift*."

4. **medley**—B: Hodgepodge; mixture of unrelated items. Old French *meslee* (mixed). "Jazz Festival Produces a *Medley* of Sound."

5. **impropriety**—A: Improper conduct; unsuitable remark. Latin *improprius* (improper). "*Improprieties* Suspected at Bridge Tournaments."

6. **quandary**—A: State of uncertainty or doubt. Perhaps a contraction of Latin *quando dare* (when to give). "Moscow Book Fair Poses *Quandary* for U.S. Publishing Houses."

7. **purge**—C: To cleanse; expel. Latin *purgare*. "Chinese *Purge* Radical Group of Four."

8. **bewail**—D: To lament; cry or complain. Middle English *biwailen*. "Consumers *Bewail* Rising Prices."

9. **renege**—B: To go back on your word; repudiate. Latin *renegare* (to deny again). "TV Star Charges Network *Reneged* on Vow."

10. **scrutinize**—C: To examine with close attention to details.

Latin *scrutari* (to search). "Mayor Promises to *Scrutinize* Budget Practices."

11. **relic**—D: Historic or sacred object. Latin *reliquiae* (remains). "Architectural *Relics* Falling Victim to Air Pollution."

12. **perky**—C: Spirited; jaunty. Perhaps from Old Norman French *perquer* (to perch). "Nation's Economy Grows More *Perky*."

13. **defector**—B: One who deserts a party or cause, especially to join the opposition. Latin *deficere* (to desert). "Soviet *Defector* Arrives in Paris."

14. **plebeian**—D: A common man. Latin *plebeius* (of the common people). "Peanut Butter, Food for *Plebeians*."

15. **monitor**—B: One who warns, reminds, advises. Latin *monere* (to warn). "Group to Act as *Monitor* of City Judicial System."

16. **composite**—A: Compound made up of various separate parts. Latin *componere* (to put together). "*Composite* Indexes Indicate Shift in Spending Priorities."

17. **scenario**—D: Synopsis of a play; screenplay; outline of proposed events or steps to accomplish an objective. Latin *scaenarium* from *scaena* (stage). "One Candidate's *Scenario* for Re-election."

18. **beguile**—C: To charm; captivate. "Miss Universe *Beguiles* City." From *be-* and *guile* (deceit); hence, the original meaning: to trick.

19. **rivet**—A: To fasten, fix, or engross one's attention. Perhaps from Latin *ripare* (to make a ship fast to the *ripa*, or shore). "Televised Sports *Rivet* Interest of Millions."

20. **remedial**—C: Supplying a remedy; often, helping to improve reading or study skills. Latin *remedium* (remedy). "Justices Order More *Remedial* Classes in Local Schools."

VOCABULARY RATINGS

20—18 correct ....exceptional
17—15 correct ....excellent
14—12 correct .... good

Neither Black Nor White

BY STUART CHASE

On a famous radio program the moderator used to hold up a ball for the studio audience to see. "What color?" he would ask. "White," they would answer. Then he turned the ball around and asked again. "Black," they said. Every question, he continued, has two sides, and we ought to hear both.

But the trouble with this is that a great many questions which perplex us today have more than two sides. Whenever we force a problem which contains various shades of gray into a rigid pattern of black or white, we create a serious roadblock to straight thinking.

John and Mary are being divorced. Their friends line up in two camps. One group declares that it is *his* fault, the other that it is *her* fault. But—perhaps both of them are to blame, or perhaps the fault lies with neither. Forces beyond the control of John and Mary may be causing them to separate—physical factors, for instance, making children an impossibility.

There are many sides to a broken marriage, not just two. All should be taken into account. Experts call this type of situation "many-valued." Many-valued questions cannot be intelligently decided on a simple either-or basis.

"Women are bad drivers!" says Roe, contemplating another bill for a crumpled fender. His friend Doe disagrees: "You're wrong. They're good drivers—better than men!"

What are the facts? Statistics of accidents indicate that in some respects women are better drivers than men, in others, worse. Women probably crumple more fenders, but mile for mile have fewer crashes involving fatal injury. The debate is meaningless as it stands—entertaining perhaps, but without profit.

Once we grasp the implications of that turning ball, we begin to watch for black-or-white arguments by others and by ourselves. We come to enjoy the mental adventure of finding them, like hidden reefs. Next we try to determine when they are warranted and when they are not.

Living things, most of us believe, are either "animal" or "vegetable." Careful biologists, however, have discovered an organism called *Euglena*, which digests food like an animal and employs photosynthesis like a plant. *Ascidians,* though classed as animals, produce cellulose, which has long been considered a unique property of plants. Either-or thinking will not fit *Euglena* or the *Ascidians*.

Similarly, the old philosophical debate, "Which shapes character—heredity or environment?" is a misleading casting of data into either-or terms. Scientists have found that *both* heredity and environment shape character. An excellent inheritance can be ruined by unfortunate associates; a mediocre collection of genes can develop, with careful upbringing, into quite a man. The pursuit of scientific truth is a many valued proposition. Scientist avoid either-or thinking.

As we tackle our personal and political problems, it helps to adopt this approach of the scientists. Black-or-white thinking can be positively dangerous in some situations. A noted columnist, for example, speaking of the part played by Nehru and other "neutralists" in the cold war, said recently: "They are not for us; therefore they are against us; therefore they are Communists." Good heavens! We have enough real Communists against us, from Leningrad to Hanoi, without taking on the whole neutralist world of perhaps a billion people!

In problems calling for specific action, the final decision may have to be a black-or-white, yes-or-no vote. But it is likely to be a wiser vote if we first review all important facts from a multivalued point of view.

Our town held a zoning hearing the other day to discuss whether a man should be allowed to open a toyshop in an area zoned for residences. The hearing quickly degenerated into a hassle between those who held that Little Business was *good* for rural towns, and those who were positive it was *bad*. The questions of how the toyshop might look, of possible hardship to the applicant, of what a zoning variance now might mean in the future—all were forgotten. The debate, stimulating as it might have been to the contestants, contributed little to an equitable solution of the specific problem before the meeting.

The current world is full of similar discussions, largely meaningless unless the variables involved are given fair consideration. You have encountered plenty of these discussions: private schools vs. public schools; city living vs. country living; amateur sports vs. professional; little business vs. big; states rights vs. federal government; freedom vs. regimentation.

This last has been around for a long time. As a two-valued debate, one side says that we must have complete freedom or submit to slavery. But a wise judge saw the trap when he remarked: "Your freedom to swing your arms ends where my nose begins." Even the most liberal society imposes restrictions on how citizens shall behave.

There are at least three good reasons why we so often accept either-or thinking:

(1) We (especially we Americans) feel that we live under pressure and must get things decided fast. "Make up your mind, Mac!"

(2) Most people are mentally lazy. It is easier to select black or white than to judge the various shades of gray. It saves analysis, fact-finding.

(3) Linguists report that the structure of the English language—indeed of all Indo-European languages—tends to

force us into the two-valued approach. We are brought up to think in opposites such as: clean vs. dirty, long vs. short, hero vs. villain, body vs. mind, true vs. false, good vs. bad, life vs. death. It takes an effort, accordingly, to bring in the intermediate tones.

But if we make the effort we shall be rewarded. We will tackle our problems more surely, and render our decisions more justly.

I Keep Hearing Voices

BY CORNELIA OTIS SKINNER

It comes as a shock suddenly to discover in oneself some eccentricity of behavior which one may have had for years without ever before being aware of it. Take voices, for instance. I find, to my fascination, that many persons, myself in particular, have a curious collection of varying voices.

I don't mean accents picked up during exposure to regional pronunciation. (I return from a trip through the South with an accent of Georgia peach-fuzz, while 24 hours in London finds me as British as a Trafalgar lion given the power of speech.) I refer to the tone and manner of delivery we use on specific occasions.

For example, the ways in which people address the elderly. It seems to be a universal conclusion that to be advanced in years means *ipso facto* to be advanced in deafness. Whoever is presented to, say, a venerable old gentleman starts conversing in a deferential bellow. The opposite approach is the hospital voice of muted concern coupled with a note of awe indicating that to grow old automatically means to grow holy.

I have a woman cousin who is a chipper 89 and when I've introduced people to her I have watched them shake her hand as if it might be a fragile bluebell and speak to her with the solemn reverence of addressing a saint not long for this world. Actually the old girl is about as fragile as a sturdy oak, has probably just downed a double whisky-sour and is rarin' to get to the Canasta table.

Certain variations in voices seem to be peculiar to male behavior—as the looking-forward-to-breakfast halloo, particularly on Pullman trains at an early hour when you're trying to sleep. As they march Indian file through your car, the leader calls out in the cry of a lumberjack poling in turbulent rapids, "OH BOY! AM I LOOKING FORWARD TO THAT CUP OF COFFEE!" Each member of the doughty crew clarions a yes siree what isn't he going to do to those ham 'n eggs, and another wants jubilantly to know what the betting is on old W. G. here having himself a big stack of pancakes.

Women are not without their own peculiar noises of enthusiasm. Take, for example, the chance meeting of former schoolmates after the hiatus of years. All of a sudden the staggering fact dawns that the one is . . . not surely *Mary Smith!!!* and the other . . . it isn't possible, *Sally Jones!!!* The emotion of recognition is expressed in the mounting melodics of gleeful and slightly hysterical sirens—and I don't refer to the sort who sat on rocks and lured mariners with dulcet sounds.

Then there is the delivery the female uses when talking to her own child in the presence of company. Plunging into a dewy-eyed motherhood act, she lilts out sweet suggestions such as "Isn't it time we went to beddy-bye?" while what she'd like to say, and what the child expects her to shrill out, is "You little pain-in-the-neck, get the hell up to bed!" Even when the child grows older the mother employs a parlance suggestive of a Victorian elocution mistress giving the proper reading of "Birds in their little nests agree." As my own son once rudely summed it up, "For Pete's sake, Mom, when you're talking about me do you have to *sing?*"

Then there is the conspiratorial voice, often used when

there is no need for secrecy, as in the case of that husband-and-wife code exchange toward the end of a social gathering: the husband rises and, in the manner of a second-story man passing the signal to his partner, mutters, "I think we'd better be . . ." and she, rising cautiously, echoes the sinister password "Yes, we'd better be . . ." What should be so hush-hush about making the simple announcement that it's late and they ought to go home?

Of the barnyard imitations and birdcalls women employ when addressing household pets, it is almost too embarrassing to speak. A shameless weakness for dogs releases from me a flow of baby talk and babbling asininities. My dogs don't seem to mind my gurgling endearments, but my family does. My parakeet voice is also pretty dreadful, being a stream of baby jargon in a falsetto soprano, giving the effect of a leaking steam valve. In fact, all domestic animals appear to reduce me to a state of infantilism, and I have even heard myself addressing a police horse as though it were swaddled in diapers and cooing in a bassinet.

I am aware that I have a voice of cheer full of ersatz sunshine that makes its nauseating appearance when I am suddenly confronted by the children of my friends—young creatures on whom I've not set eyes for years. This voice with hypocritical eagerness utters banalities like "How's the new math teacher?" or "Your dad says you're coming along just fine with your surfboard!"

Only a week ago I shared a train seat with an attractive young woman who turned out to be the daughter of former neighbors. I didn't recognize her until she introduced herself saying that she was Penelope E. I immediately came out with a loud "Why Penny *Pen!*" and pumping her hand with splendid vigor exclaimed, "Last time I saw you, you were covered with poison ivy!" What she was covered with then was discomfort. Obviously she hadn't been called by the distressing nickname in years. However, she smiled indulgently and replied politely to my elephantine inquiries as to how was the family, did she enjoy school and mercy it wasn't possible that she had graduated from *college!* Shortly Penny Pen, under pretext of smoking a cigarette, sought refuge in another car.

Another locution I have recently discovered is my doctor

voice. Not the confiding mutter used in situations of illness or consultation, but the one I catch myself using when I meet one of the medical profession socially. Possibly out of a desire to give the impression that I have no need for his professional services, I talk with great animation in tones vibrant with radiant health. If he happens to be a psychiatrist also, I have the disquieting feeling that the chair I am sitting on is about to let down into a couch and that my every gesture is indicative of deep-rooted neuroses. The result is a careful enunciation to show how frightfully normal I am.

However, there is nothing to equal my talking-with-a-foreigner delivery. And I do not refer to someone who speaks only a foreign tongue, with whom one decides the only means of communication is through a bellow of English. I mean the cultured linguist who speaks my language with far greater elegance than I. If through the perfection of his Oxford verbiage there comes the slightest hint of foreign accent, I slow down to LP speed, mouthing each syllable with meticulous deliberation and using the basic words of a *First Primer*. It is the form of painstaking peroration William Penn must have used when explaining his treaty to the Indians.

Then there is my chatting-with-clergymen parlance. The sudden sight of a clerical collar makes me go right into my voice of piety: a combination of the hostess of a Cape Cod tea shoppe and Beth in *Little Women*, hushed and not a little hallowed, as though we were about to step into the next room and view the remains. It is somewhat reassuring to note that others carry on conversations with parsons in the same funereal manner. It must be one of the more doleful exactions of the dedicated life.

Finally there is my losing-interest voice, which is less a voice than a fade-out. This creeps slowly upon me during some interminable tête-à-tête with, say, a golf enthusiast or someone just back from Europe and determined to present an unillustrated travelogue. What issues from my mouth is quite mechanical; in fact, I usually have no idea what I am saying. This is disturbing for it creates that eerie sensation of standing outside yourself and listening to a complete stranger.

This listening to myself is making me uncomfortably self-conscious. Perhaps I had better stop enumerating all my varying forms of speech.

Perhaps, as a matter of fact, in certain situations it might be best for me to stop speaking altogether.

Word Power Test No. 15

The Sporting Life

BY PETER FUNK

In this selection of words from the sports columns of the daily press, check the word or phrase you believe is *nearest in meaning* to the key word. Answers are at the end of this test.

1. **effectuate** (ĕ fek′ tū āt)—A: to accomplish. B: begin. C: practice. D: end.

2. **perceptive** (per sep′ tiv)—A: wise. B: alert. C: discerning. D: precise.

3. **syndrome** (sin′ drōm)—A: council. B: combination of symptoms. C: fetish. D: monopoly.

4. **fastidious** (fas tid′ ĭ us)—A: revelation. B: pithy saying. C: perfect example. D: fussy.

5. **apotheosis** (a poth ē ō′ sis)—A: revelation. B: pithy saying. C: perfect example. D: rhetorical address.

6. **pristine** (pris′ tēn; pris tēn′)—A: beautiful. B: prudish. C: shining. D: fresh and untouched.

7. **forbearance** (for bear′ ans)—A: patience. B: foresight. C: stubbornness. D: inherited traits.

8. **codicil** (cod′ uh s′l)—A: tabulation. B: summary. C: supplement. D: international agreement.

9. **hybrid** (hī′ brid)—A: pure. B: carefully selected. C: mixed. D: hardy.

10. **sully** (sul′ ē)—A: to ridicule. B: leap forth. C: deceive. D: tarnish.

11. **blatant** (blā′ tant)—A: conceited. B: unpleasantly noisy. C: brutal. D: openly hostile.

12. **sanguinary** (sang′ gwĭ nair ē)—A: optimistic. B: listless. C: overwhelming. D: bloody.

13. **peregrination** (per ĕ grĭ nā′ shun)—A: land measurement. B: uncertainty. C: travel. D: scheme.

14. **obloquy** (ob′ lō kwē)—A: abusive language. B: state of being forgotten. C: discussion. D: burial rite.

15. **mettle** (met′ ′l)—A: mood. B: courage. C: sternness. D: belligerence.

16. **infraction** (in frak′ shun)—A: small portion. B: collision. C: oversight. D: violation.

17. **lethal** (lē′ thal)—A: deadly. B: mean. C: murky. D: heavy.

18. **contemptuous** (kon temp′ tū us)—A: cynical. B: scornful. C: arrogant. D: uncivil.

19. **perennial** (per en′ ĭ al)—A: early. B: infrequent. C: persistent. D: spreading.

20. **finesse** (fĭ nĕs′)—A: sleight of hand. B: insight. C: ending. D: skill.

ANSWERS

1. **effectuate**—A: To accomplish; bring about; as, to *effectuate* changes in spring-training rules. Latin *efficere*.

2. **perceptive**—C: Discerning; sensitive; capable of sympathetic understanding intuitively or through keen observation; as, a *perceptive* coach. Latin *percipere* (to feel, grasp).

3. **syndrome**—B: Combination of symptoms characteristic of a particular abnormality; as, a pitcher's shoulder-arm *syndrome*. Greek *syndromē*.

4. **fastidious**—D: Fussy; hard to please; overly exacting; as, *fastidious* attention to details. Latin *fastidiosus*.

5. **apotheosis**—C: Perfect example; highest development; final form; as, the *apotheosis* of versatility. Greek *apotheōsis*, from *apotheoun* (to deify).

6. **pristine**—D: Fresh and untouched; unspoiled; unpolluted; primitive; as, a *pristine* trout stream. Latin *pristinus* (early).

7. **forbearance**—A: Patience; self-control; restraint; leniency; as, to view minor offenses with *forbearance*. Old English *forberan*.

8. **codicil**—C: A supplement; usually a later addition to a will, modifying or revoking it. Latin *codex* (a book made of wood blocks).

9. **hybrid**—C: Mixed; blended; composed of diverse elements; as, platform tennis—a *hybrid* derivative of tennis, jai alai

and ballroom dancing. Latin *hybrida* (offspring of a mixed union).

10. **sully**—D: To tarnish; stain; blemish; as, to *sully* the team's record. French *souiller* (to soil).

11. **blatant**—B: Unpleasantly noisy; loud and vulgar; as, a *blatant* crowd of spectators. Latin *blatire* (to chatter).

12. **sanguinary**—D: Bloody; marked by bloodshed; as, a *sanguinary* free-for-all. Latin *sanguis* (blood).

13. **peregrination**—C: Travel; wandering; as, the basketball team's early *peregrination*. Latin *peregrinari* (to travel).

14. **obloquy**—A: Abusive language; public defamation; calumny; as, to heap *obloquy* on the referee. Latin *obloqui* (to speak against, abuse, chide).

15. **mettle**—B: Courage; spirit; stamina; as, to test a rookie's *mettle*. Middle English *metel* (metal, mettle).

16. **infraction**—D: Violation; breaking; as, an *infraction* of racing regulations. Latin *infringere* (to break off).

17. **lethal**—A: Deadly; fatal; devastating; as a *lethal* southpaw. Latin *letum* (death).

18. **contemptuous**—B: Scornful; showing disdain or contempt; as, to be *contemptuous* of the hecklers. Latin *contemptus*.

19. **perennial**—C: Persistent; enduring; recurring regularly; as, *perennial* champions. Latin *perennis* (lasting).

20. **finesse**—D: Delicate skill or artistry in performance; adroit maneuvering in a difficult situation; as, a hockey player's *finesse*. Middle French *fin* (fine).

VOCABULARY RATINGS

20—18 correct ....exceptional
17—15 correct ....excellent
14—12 correct .... good

The Delicate Art of Asking Questions

BY JOHN KORD LAGEMANN

For getting to the heart of the matter, professionals have developed special skills and techniques invaluable to everyone

Americans, it has been said, fondly believe they have three natural-born skills—making love, playing poker and interviewing. The fact is, however, that each of these "natural" skills can be improved. And not the least to benefit by study and application is the last: the art of obtaining information.

No matter who we are or what our way of life, it has become increasingly important to discover what people feel and think—about almost every subject under the sun. When we hire someone or apply for a job, when we discuss our work with a boss or a subordinate, when we see our doctor, our banker or the children's teacher, we interview and are interviewed. Even when we talk with husband, wife, children, friends, we are often in the position of the interviewer, trying to get beneath the surface and find out what *really* happened or what someone *really* thinks.

How can we do this more successfully? A number of techniques, developed by experts, are useful:

RECOGNIZE THAT EVERY ENCOUNTER IS "EMOTIONAL." There is no such thing as an impersonal meeting of minds. Look inward: there's a human awareness, an exchange of feelings, with the waiter who takes your luncheon order, the clerk who adds up your bill at the supermarket, the unseen person at the other end of a telephone wire. (Witness the difference, the *im*personality of it, when the telephone voice turns out to be recorded.)

But to enter into any real give-and-take we have to let down our defenses. "Every human encounter is an emotional experience in which we risk some of our self-esteem," said the pioneer psychiatrist Dr. Harry Stack Sullivan. "Under stress of that anxiety, people may become suspicious or resentful or downright hostile."

How can we penetrate this defensiveness and find the answers we seek?

MAKE YOUR PURPOSE CLEAR. "When you start asking questions," says the noted pollster Dr. George Gallup, "the other person immediately wonders, 'Why does he want to know?' Unless your purpose is clear, he may be reluctant to talk or he may seize the opportunity to tell you all about his problems."

When you go to your doctor for an examination, the situation is self-defined and the doctor can ask you intimate questions which you would resent from anyone else. In applying for a loan, though, you accept questions from a banker that you would resent from your doctor. It's a matter of defining the situation, and a clearly understood agenda lessens the natural anxiety that otherwise impedes the flow of information.

How often have you said, "But why didn't you *tell* me what you were after?" Once at a party someone I'd never seen before started questioning me about an old friend. How long had I known him? What did I think of this and that thing he had done? When I asked a little huffily what business he had checking up, he said, "Oh, Lord, didn't you know? I'm his brother!"

RESPOND TO EXPRESSIONS OF FEELING. This is a powerful tool which many professional counselors—clinical psychologists, doctors, ministers—have learned to use in getting to the bottom of personal problems that people bring to them. Instead of trying to reassemble the facts (who said or did what to whom) or to give specific advice, they listen for and encourage all expressions of feeling, however faint or fleeting. Statements that begin "I feel" or "I wish" or "I don't care if," the interviewer acknowledges, perhaps by repeating their content. Or he may just note, "You feel very strongly about that, don't you?" or "Is that so?" Having such feelings recognized, without judgment or criticism, often has an almost magical effect in making a person open up. The truth comes out, and with it, often, self-insight.

A friend in the hospital told me about one of his roommates, Sanderson, who had upset the whole floor with his constant petty complaints and even threats of lawsuit. The head nurse and the resident doctor tried to question him in detail about his grievances but could get nowhere. Finally an intern got to the root of the trouble.

"They don't care what happens to me," Sanderson said.

Quietly, the intern rephrased the statement: "It seems to you the nurses don't really care."

"It's as if the whole world had turned against me," Sanderson said.

"It makes you feel lonely," said the intern, again responding to the feeling instead of impatiently brushing it aside to get at "the facts."

That was what the patient needed, someone who paid attention not merely to his ailments but to *him*. He opened up and talked at length. Most of the things that annoyed him were trifles, and, now that someone understood, the unavoidable inconveniences no longer upset him.

People skilled in human relations—notably, those women credited with "feminine intuition"—have always used this potent technique of listening for emotional overtones. Often in this way they achieve a true understanding so fast that it baffles the purely fact-oriented.

LEARN THE ART OF OPEN-END. Don't ask too many questions. Instead of the cross-examination approach, professional interviewers nowadays often start just by getting people talking—about the weather, sports, anything. And for depth interviewing they have developed the open-end question, which does not restrict the other person but lets him assume the initiative and carry the conversation wherever he likes.

A teacher I had in college used this technique skillfully

to release ideas and talents within his students. Instead of just lecturing, he would bring up a point developed in something we'd read, then ask one of us, "How about that?" or "What do you think?" By responding with an occasional "hmm," or a flickering smile or a puzzled frown, he would keep us on that elusive rainbow path that leads to an original idea. We frequently had the experience of discovering that we knew more than we thought we knew.

DON'T TELL THE OTHER PERSON WHAT TO SAY. According to expert pollsters, "feedback" from the interviewer's own predilections or wishes is the greatest single source of error in public-opinion polls. Quite unconsciously we throw out clues that suggest what we want people to say. That's why a top executive often has a hard time avoiding yes-men. Fathers often run into the same trouble when they try to find out just what their children are up to.

"In polls, some of the best respondents are teen-agers," says Pearl Zinner, of the National Opinion Research Center of the University of Chicago. "This always amazes parents, who say, 'They never talk to *us* that openly.' The reason frequently is, of course, that the children feel they must doctor reports of their thoughts and activities, to avoid unpleasantness."

WATCH YOUR WORDING. Finding in the other person just what you expected to find usually means that you are putting words into his mouth. At a birthday party for eight-year-olds, I saw the guest of honor reach for the last piece of candy while asking, "Nobody wants any more candy, do they?" Adults are hardly more subtle.

Because of this human tendency, "question building" for professional polls has become an art in itself. "Tricky or badly constructed questions can push or mislead others into giving completely false answers," says Stanley L. Payne, author of the book *The Art of Asking Questions*.

Suppose you are measuring opinion for and against a certain political project. You could ask, "Should the state issue bonds for the money?" Or you could ask, "Should the state go into debt for this?" As Payne points out, both may present the issue accurately, but one question is loaded to produce favorable answers, the other to arouse opposition.

A name can inject an emotional charge into an issue. "Do you agree with President Johnson (or Eisenhower) that . . ." is one way of loading a question. "Do you agree with the Red Chinese that . . ." is loaded to draw a high percentage of "No" answers. Questions that ask if people are *for* something always get more favorable answers than those which ask if they are against something.

PROTECT THE OTHER PERSON. Detective novels and courtroom dramas usually show an interview as a duel of wits in which the object is to probe for the other person's weak spots. In real life, detectives, lawyers, social workers and others who have to ask for sensitive information generally follow the opposite rule—they lead to strength. The reason: looking for weaknesses always puts the other person's guard up. Recognizing a strength creates a bond.

Protecting the other person's pride is a vital part of getting information. As economist Stuart Chase points out, "Veteran interviewers in an unemployment survey would never ask, 'You're not working now, are you?' but rather 'Are you looking for a job right now, or waiting for a while?'" An expert marriage counselor does not ask, "What do you and your wife quarrel about?" but, "When conflicts arise, how do you try to settle them?"

START WHERE THE OTHER PERSON IS. "Beginners," says Dr. Leslie A. Osborn of the University of Nebraska College of Medicine, "often rush into an area of feeling where the other person is not yet ready to admit them. They sometimes build up so much resistance they never even get close."

A worried heart patient, for example, may have to discuss the effects of his illness on his work and his family before he can plunge into an objective discussion of symptoms. A woman preoccupied with immediate problems of children and household cannot be expected to shift focus instantly and give a pollster meaningful views on foreign policy or abstract art. It is up to the interviewer to find out what is on the other person's mind and to start from there, for the shortest distance between two subjects or points of view may well be the long way around.

The successful interview, more like a good conversation than an interrogation, leaves the interviewed person feeling somehow heartened and uplifted. Why? Red Barber, after 30 years of successful interviewing for radio and TV, says, "The Greeks had a word for it—*agape* (ah′ gah pā). It's one of the most wonderful words man possesses, and it means broadly 'to have concern for'."

To have concern for the other person, and show it, is the rule that makes all the others work.

The Baffling World of Psychobabble

BY R. D. ROSEN

A new style of talk is abroad in the land, and the more it says the less it seems to mean

Confession is the new handshake.

These days it seems that everyone belongs to the cult of candor, that everything must be spoken and that everyone speaks the same dialect. Are you relating? Good. Are you getting in touch with yourself? Fine. Exactly how heavy are those changes you're going through? Doing your own thing? Is your head screwed on straight? Are you going to get your act together? Are you a whole person or only a fraction thereof?

One hears it everywhere, like endless panels of a Jules Feiffer cartoon. In restaurants, distraught lovers lament, "I just wish I could get into your head." A man on a bus turns to his companion and says, "I just got back from the Coast. What a different headset!" A California group therapist intones, "You gotta be you 'cause you're you and you gotta be, and besides, if you aren't gonna be you who else's gonna be you, honey? This is the Aquarian Age and the time to be yourself, to love one's beauty, to go with one's process."

Let's call this psychological patter "psychobabble," a spirit which tyrannized conversation in the 1970s. It is difficult to avoid, and there is often an embarrassment involved in not using it, somewhat akin to the mild humiliation experienced in Paris by American tourists who cannot speak the native tongue. Psychobabble is now spoken by magazine editors, management consultants, sandal makers, tool and die workers, chiefs of state, Ph.D.s in clinical psychology, and just about everyone else.

Its specific origins can only be hinted at. On one level, it seems to have emerged toward the end of the '60s, distilled from the dying radical/liberal dialects of activism and confrontation, absorbing some black-ghetto phrases along the way. But its roots are also planted in today's popular therapies—encounter groups, sensitivity training, primal scream, etc.

Of course, this is not the first time in our history that psychological ideas have so dominated national conversation. Previously, in the '40s and '50s, Freudian terms—repression, sublimation, wish fulfillment and the like—were glibly used by people as if they really understood Freud and what he was talking about.

The new psychobabblers, however, don't even seem to know the *terms* of Freudian or any other organized body of psychological theory. Their jargon seems to free-float in an all-purpose linguistic atmosphere, killing off the very spontaneity, candor and understanding it pretends to promote.

Uptight, for instance, is a word used to describe an individual experiencing anything from mild uneasiness to a clinical depression. To ask someone why he or she refers to another as being *hung up* elicits a reply that reveals neither understanding nor curiosity: "Well, you know, he's just, well, hung up."

And the terms are used recklessly. One is no longer fearful; one is *paranoid*. Increasingly, people describe their moody acquaintances as *manic-depressives,* and almost anyone you don't like is *psychotic* or at the very least *schized-out*.

Many people express the view that this new psychobabble is a constructive retreat from obfuscating clinical terms. But, if so, it is only a retreat into a sweet banality, a sort of syrup poured over conversations to make them go down easier.

What appears to be occurring in the therapeutic culture of the '70s is the suppression of natural declarative speech itself, the suppression of language in its richest, most associative, most unpredictable, revealing, hence therapeutic, form. The erosion of written and spoken English has been widely documented during the last several years, but perhaps nowhere does that damage seem more inhibiting than in the way some people talk—or rather fail to talk—about themselves.

Psychobabble represents the rejection of narration in favor of psychological ad copy:

"I'm really into my anger right now," she says.

"That's okay," he replies. "That's your space. Go with the anger."

"Yeah, but I feel a lot of hostility toward you and I feel that I want to get that out."

"That's cool. That's the space you're in. I can understand exactly where you're coming from. I've been there."

"Still, you've really been on my case and I have all this anger that I want to share with you."

"Like I said, that's cool. I want to tell you that I acknowledge your anger and that I acknowledge you."

"Good, I get that it's okay to be angry with you."

Consider for a moment a society in which psychobabble has become what passes for ordinary language. Anyone left in this society with an ear for nuance and a sense of history would have a harder and harder time trying to elicit what used to be called *meaning* from the reign of platitudes. The modern range of experience, far from being expanded, would be diminished by the prevalence of verbal labels.

In a world dominated by psychobabble, everyone would be getting their empty heads together in the intolerably banal here and now. Everyone would be engaged in a sort of perpetual emotional filibuster unconsciously designed to prevent any real issues from coming to a vote.

It probably will go away eventually. Unfortunately, in

the meantime, attempts at real dialogue often turn into psychobabble. Let's get back to self-awareness, psychological responsibility and the central importance of language.

Word Power Test No. 16

How Cicero Made Adjectives

BY PETER FUNK

When a Roman orator like Cicero wanted to turn a Latin verb into an adjective, he used an ending that has come down to us as "-ant" or "-ent," depending on the spelling of the original verb. Each adjective in the test below has one or the other of these endings, each intended to show that some action or quality is being described. It takes a skillful speller to keep "-ant" words and "-ent" words straight—but that's a tax we're still paying to the language of ancient Rome. Check the word or phrase that you believe is *nearest in meaning* to the key word below. Answers appear at the end of this test.

1. **stagnant** (stag′ nant)—A: muddy. B: quiet. C: oppressive. D: stale or foul.
2. **fervent** (fer′ vent)—A: enthusiastic. B: languid. C: restless. D: impressionable.
3. **reticent** (ret′ uh sent)—A: aloof. B: uncertain. C: modest. D: reserved.
4. **indolent** (in′ duh lent)—A: lenient. B: lazy. C: easygoing. D: diligent.
5. **belligerent** (bě lij′ uh rent)—A: hostile. B: cranky. C: noisy. D: insulting.
6. **flagrant** (flā′ grant)—A: aromatic. B: openly scandalous. C: spiteful. D: careless.
7. **insolent** (in′ sŏ lent)—A: conciliatory. B: coarse. C: caustically witty. D: haughty and contemptuous.
8. **apparent** (ă pâr′ ent)—A: obvious. B: tentative. C: explicit. D: illusory.
9. **nascent** (nā′ sent)—A: knowledgeable. B: starting to develop. C: unlimited. D: aged.
10. **dormant** (dor′ mant)—A: relaxed. B: hidden. C: peaceful. D: inactive.

11. **fragrant** (frā′ grant)—A: sweet-smelling. B: fractional. C: noisome. D: delicate.

12. **insolvent** (in sŏl′ vent)—A: difficult to solve. B: unsettled. C: bankrupt. D: sticky.

13. **translucent** (trans lu′ sent)—A: murky. B: crystalline. C: pure. D: semi-transparent.

14. **pertinent** (pur′ tĭ nent)—A: relevant. B: auxiliary. C: quick to respond. D: cheerful.

15. **indignant** (in dig′ nant)—A: angry. B: touchy. C: informal. D: cordial.

16. **fluent** (flū′ ent)—A: speaking easily. B: indecisive. C: changeable. D: highly intelligent.

17. **migrant** (mī′ grant)—A: restless. B: poor. C: shiftless. D: wandering.

18. **exorbitant** (eg zor′ bĭ tant)—A: threatening. B: excessive. C: ridiculous. D: odd.

19. **prudent** (prōō′ dent)—A: flamboyant. B: fussy. C: overly modest or proper. D: wisely careful.

20. **benevolent** (bĕ nĕv′ uh lent)—A: thoughtful. B: cheerful. C: kind. D: wrathful.

ANSWERS

1. **stagnant**—D: Stale or foul; lacking vitality; as, *stagnant* water, or a *stagnant* imagination. The Latin *stagnare* means to form a pool. (All of these test words come from Latin.)

2. **fervent**—A: Enthusiastic. *Fervere* (to glow or boil). When you experience a *fervent* desire, you have an intense warmth of feeling or great zeal.

3. **reticent**—D: Reserved; saying little; as, "The statesman was *reticent* about his private life." *Reticere* (to keep silent).

4. **indolent**—B: Lazy; disliking work. From *in-* (not) and *dolere* (to suffer pain). Perhaps an insight into how the ancients viewed work!

5. **belligerent**—A: Aggressively hostile or fond of fighting; warlike; as, "A *belligerent* attitude makes peace negotiations difficult." *Bellum* (war) and *gerere* (to wage).

6. **flagrant**—B: Openly scandalous or disgraceful; notorious. *Flagare* (to blaze, glow). A flame is easily seen; thus, a *flagrant* disregard for the law is clearly visible.

7. **insolent**—D: Haughty and contemptuous; disrespectful; as, "The *insolent* tax official irritated everyone." *Insolescere* (to become haughty).

8. **apparent**—A: Obvious; plain to see; easily perceived; as, "The poet's wife was his *apparent* inspiration." *Apparere* (to become visible).

9. **nascent**—B: Just starting to develop. *Nasci* (to be born). A *nascent* idea, therefore, is one that just came to mind.

10. **dormant**—D: Inactive. *Dormire* (to sleep). Hence, a *dormant* volcano, or a *dormant* talent, is "sleeping" or quiescent.

11. **fragrant**—A: Sweet-smelling; having a pleasant odor; as, a *fragrant* rose. *Fragrare* (to emit an odor).

12. **insolvent**—C: Bankrupt. *Solvere* first meant "to set free." So, if a person is *insolvent*, he is "not free," but bound by his debts.

13. **translucent**—D: Semi-transparent; letting light pass, but diffusing it so that objects on the opposite side cannot be distinguished. Frosted glass is *translucent*. *Translucere* (to shine through), from *trans* (across) and *lucere* (to shine).

14. **pertinent**—A: Relevant; related to the matter being considered; apt; as, a *pertinent* question. *Pertinere* (to reach to).

15. **indignant**—A: Angry at whatever is unjust, unfair or disgraceful; as, an *indignant* speech. Late Latin *indignari* (to be angry because of some unworthy act).

16. **fluent**—A: Speaking easily. *Fluere* means "to flow." When you speak or write *fluently,* your words flow smoothly and easily.

17. **migrant**—D: Wandering; roving; a *migrant* worker moves from place to place. *Migrare* (to migrate).

18. **exorbitant**—B: Excessive beyond what is normally expected and proper; extravagant; as, *exorbitant* demands. Church Latin *exorbitare* (to deviate) comes from *ex* (out) and *orbita* (wheel-rut, track).

19. **prudent**—D: Wisely careful. A *prudent* administrator is cautious, discreet, foresighted. *Providere* (to see at a distance).

20. **benevolent**—C: Kind, generous; desiring whatever is good for others. *Bene* (well) and *velle* (to wish). A *benevolent* uncle wishes you well.

VOCABULARY RATINGS

20—18 correct ....exceptional
17—15 correct ....excellent
14—12 correct .... good

Oh, Waddle I Do?

A plaintive plea for rediscovery of the lost art of diction

BY JANET AGLE

Only yesterday (when I was a child) enunciation was given rigorous attention. Woe betide the child, for instance, who failed to sound the first "c" in arctic! Now diction is one of the lost arts—and the problem is at its most acute with my own children.

The boys were watching television the other day when the phone rang. "Dad says dough way form," one of them reported. "Sgonna be late."

When the children were younger, I thought indulgently that age would cure their difficulties, and I looked forward to the time when we could exchange thoughts freely. Now it is apparent that the situation has worsened alarmingly.

An uncle gave one of the boys a present. "Gee!" said my son happily. "He sure is a jenner sky!" (My child feels sorry for kids who don't have any answer uncles.)

To follow our boys' games you need a special glossary. They play war with mock hang gernades. Sometimes they knock out the turt gunner, but usually someone escapes in a pair shoot. For ammunition they use tense balls.

My difficulties are not confined to my own family. The taxi driver says that he'll stop in front of the lawner mat. The cleaning woman announces that a tradesman cheed her of a dollar. It is strange, I'm told, that the salesgirl cannot be found; she was there a mindigo.

Everywhere our language is being whittled down; old, familiar syllables have disappeared. Consider "just." "He sleft," for instance, or, "I swashed my hair and can't do a thing with it." And "have not" is almost obsolete. "I ham seenum," the doctor's secretary told me this morning. "I sgot here myself."

I was relieved when the College of Carnals, having selected a new Pope, was not heard of so frequently. But I still jump when the butcher suggests poorhouse steak.

I am a voice in the wilderness, and my cry is always the same: an incredulous *"What?"*

My husband gives me little sympathy. "Try paying attention," he suggested recently.

"Oh, waddle I do?" I said suddenly. "Half the time I canner stand what's going on."

"What?"

I looked at him coldly. "Smatter?" I asked. "Can CHEER me?"

Why Did They Call It *That*?

BY GARY JENNINGS

The English who scratched out the early settlements on the eastern rim of this continent—my own ancestors among them—all seem to have been hungry, thirsty, weary or peevish. It shows in the place names they foisted on us. Witness the several Bread Loaf and Sugar Loaf Mountains, Martha's Vineyard, Cape Comfort, Troublesome Creek. Stingray Point got its name when Capt. John Smith foolishly picked up a live sting ray—and regretted it. The colonists were plain people, and given to plain juiceless names like Skinquarter and Mulch (in Virginia), Buzzard's Bay, and mountains called Pignut, Wart and Pimple.

Other expatriate Englishmen, knowing which side of the ocean their bread was buttered on, named settlements for kings, queens and princelings—or creditors. Still others, homesick, used the names of the towns they had left. Norfolk, New Castle, Southampton—all yearningly face namesakes across the water.

Many an American community still wobbles under the

weight of an erroneous or ambiguous appellation. Massachusetts owes its Marblehead to some marblehead who couldn't recognize the rock as granite. In Iowa there is a little town called Mystic. Nothing occult about it, just a tidied-up rendition of the remark made by the first migrants who came there to work the coal mines: "This is a *mistake* ." The harbor city of Newport News, Va., whose name puzzles everybody, was originally the new (or second) port founded by the brothers Newce.

Stephen Vincent Benét, who wrote, "I have fallen in love with American names, the sharp names that never get fat," had to delve deep inland to find sharp names like Medicine Hat, Deadwood and Lost Mule Flat. The trappers, traders, scouts and prospectors who escaped westward from the sissy East called a spade a spade, and a mountain shaped like an outhouse, Outhouse Mountain. To them we owe Death Valley, Hungry Horse, Massacre Rocks, Gouge Eye, Rum River, Gunsight Hills. Yet not all of their names were riproarers; some have the ring of discovery, or the reminiscence of a lifesaving oasis, or the serenity of the whispering wilderness—Bonanza, Eureka, Sweetwater, Sweetgrass, Ten Sleep, Sleepy Eye and Dreaming Creek.

Inevitably the civilizers and the nice-namers moved in, and some sharp names got jettisoned for the sake of "progress." Scranton doesn't sound like much of a refinement unless you know that it once suffered under the rousing cognomen of Skunk's Misery. Portsmouth, N.H., before it genuflected to the original in England, was Strawberry Bank. But Marthasville, Ga., didn't lose anything when the Western & Atlantic Railroad picked it for a terminus and insisted it adopt the coined name of Atlanta. And New York's Storm King Mountain certainly sounds more rugged and Peer Gyntish than it did as Butter Hill.

Several years ago the crossroads hamlet of Tightsqueeze, Va., changed its name to Fairview. The citizens, thrilled at having got into the news for probably the first time in history, immediately switched the name back to Tightsqueeze and thereby got into the news again.

Toward the close of the 19th century, when the pesky Indians had all but vanished, America suddenly decided that their venerable languages would make splendid new place names. But these tongues feature thorny hedges of consonants separated by gutters of grunts. The noble Red Man would never recognize some of the "Indian" names on the map today.

Translating the original lingo into such license-plate poetry as Land of the Sky-Blue Waters calls for considerable contortions, because the Indian words seldom meant anything poetic. Mississippi means not Father of Waters but only Big River; Chesapeake means the same; both Ohio and Allegheny mean simply Good Waters. The Ojibwa's word *she-ka-gong*, or Chicago, meant Stinking River. If the Indian words had any semantic virtue, it lay in their occasional portmanteau capacity. For instance, Stuykson (Tucson) somehow managed to mean Village of the shaded Spring at the Foot of the Mountains.

More evocative than the English are the mellifluous names of the French-explored fringes and the far Southwest where the Spanish settled. A French trapper could be confronted by a forbidding escarpment of Wyoming crags and somehow be reminded of his mistress's grand *tétons* —while one of Shakespeare's countrymen, roaming the gentle Blue Ridge, could come upon a truly lovely-shaped hill and see only a Hogback. Where the Franciscan would find an *arroyo,* or the Jesuit a *coulée,* the Puritan espied a plain gully. If the Spanish had not inspired the sonorous name, Grand Canyon, we would probably be calling it today That Ditch.

Of course the conquistadores and missionaries weren't infallibly imaginative. Both French and Spanish explorers were wont to name a new place for the saint on whose day it was discovered. But under the sun of southern California those soft Sans and Santas—Ynez, Ysabel, Juan de Capistrano—seem irreplaceably right. When our third-largest city was just a flyspeck on the map, it bore the wonderfully resounding title of El Pueblo de Nuestra Señora la Reina de Los Angeles de Porciúncula—The Town of Our Lady the Queen of the Angels of the Little Allotment of Land. And now we clip it in the slothful modern manner to a contemptuous L.A.!

A French or Spanish place name in America, though it may be simply descriptive, has a glamour lacking in its English counterpart. Prairie du Chien is a much swanker address than would be Dog Field, Wis. The Malheur River is more inviting than it would be as the Bad Luck River. Boca Raton, however it got the name, is easier for the Florida Chamber of Commerce to promote than Mouse Mouth would be.

In some places, a foreign name has stuck unrecognized. Ozark is simply a phonetic spelling of Aux Arks—a clipped French expression meaning "at the place of the Arkansa tribe." And the Lemon Fair River was named by a Vermonter trying to pronounce Les Monts Verts.

A handful of Dutch place names around Nieuw Amsterdam, or New York, still glitter with originality: the Murderkill River, memorializing an Indian fight; Hell Gate, or Hellegat; and Spuyten Duyvil Creek, where a Hollander swore he would swim the dangerous crossing "in spite of the devil."

By way of contrast, consider the prosaic names inflicted in more "enlightened" times—from Ada, Okla., to Zook, Kan. Pennsylvania has enshrined the sooty god Industry in such towns as Trucksville and Factoryville. The demon Yaketty-Yak is evidently worshiped in both Telegraph and Telephone, Texas. And in 1950, Hot Springs, N.M., convulsed itself into Truth or Consequences.

The logical conclusion is that we might improve the whole map by wiping it clean and starting over. Perhaps hold contests for the best name to replace Ho-ho-kus, N.J., or Weed, Calif. And yet . . . and yet there are at least a couple of classic, high-sounding names worth preserving. In the course of my research for this article, I found there is a community named Gary in each of six states and a Jennings in eight.

Word Power Test No. 17

Political Vocabulary

BY PETER FUNK

Every occupation has its particular vocabulary, and politics is no exception. During elections, certain words crop up more frequently than at other times. If you were listening to a candidate and the following 20 words were used, how many of them would you know? Check the word or phrase you believe is *nearest in meaning* to the key word. Answers are at the end of this test.

1. **ethnic** (eth' nik)—of or relating to A: principles. B: discrimination. C: nationality or race. D: medicine.
2. **faction** (făk' shun)—pertaining to A: inflexibility. B: a majority. C: clique. D: influence.
3. **anachronistic** (ă nak rŏ nis' tik)—A: specialized. B: political. C: out-of-date. D: odd.
4. **ideology** (i dē ŏl' ō jē)—A: creativeness. B: image worship. C: unquestioning trust. D: beliefs.
5. **contender** (kon tend' er)—one who A: accuses. B: demands. C: defies. D: competes.
6. **incumbent** (in kum' bent)—A: oppressor. B: negotiator. C: officeholder. D: critic.
7. **acclamation** (ak lă mā' shun)—A: agreement. B: adaptation. C: gathering. D: wild applause.
8. **fratricide** (frat' rĭ sīd)—A: meeting of like-minded persons. B: being on friendly terms. C: act of killing a brother. D: exaggerated patriotism.
9. **Populist** (pop' ū list)—A: rural progressive. B: political straddler. C: conformist. D: birth-control advocate.
10. **mandate** (man' dāt)—A: deadline. B: authoritative order. C: clearly defined position. D: strong inclination.
11. **consensus** (kon sen' sus)—A: general agreement. B: summary. C: official count. D: recommendation.

12. **disavow** (dis ă vow')—A: to repudiate. B: lie. C: condemn. D: insist.

13. **gerrymander** (jer' ē man der)—A: to alter unfairly. B: invalidate. C: make excuses. D: be fickle.

14. **demagogue** (dem' ă gog)—A: sovereign. B: one advocating violence. C: dictator. D: political agitator.

15. **telegenic** (tel ĕ jen' ik)—A: scientifically inclined. B: attractive on television. C: farsighted. D: disinterested.

16. **bloc**—A: group. B: obstacle. C: diagram. D: formation.

17. **polarization** (pō lar ĭ zā' shun)—A: neutralizing force. B: related to the arctic. C: a gathering around opposing extremes. D: fluctuation.

18. **junket** (jun' kit)—A: illegal practice. B: travel. C: short speech. D: ineffective legislation.

19. **pork barrel**—A: emergency policy. B: free gifts. C: cribes and graft. D: funds for local improvements.

20. **radical** (răd' ĭ k'l)—one who is A: extreme. B: unreasonable. C: an anarchist. D: dangerous.

ANSWERS

1. **ethnic**—C: Relating to nationality or race, or to characteristics of people possessing a common heritage; as, Irish, Negro, Polish and other *ethnic* groups. Greek *ethnos* (race, tribe).

2. **faction**—C: A clique working for its own ends; as, a new sense of coöperation between party *factions*. Latin *factio* (a making or doing).

3. **anachronistic**—C: Out-of-date; belonging to a former age and now inappropriate. Greek *anachronizein* (to refer to a wrong time).

4. **ideology**—D: Beliefs and ideas that form the basis of a political, economic or social system; as, "He appears *ideologically* elusive." French *idéologie*.

5. **contender**—D: One who competes for position; as, "This man is the best-qualified *contender*." Latin *contendere* (to strain, exert).

6. **incumbent**—C: Currently in office; as, the *incumbent* President. Latin *incumbere* (to lie or lean upon).

7. **acclamation**—D: Wild applause; as, "The Presidential candidate was nominated by *acclamation*." Latin *acclamare* (to cry out).

8. **fratricide**—C: Killing a brother, relative, countryman; as, "The party engaged in *fratricide* over the choice of a nominee." Latin *fratricida*, from *frater* (brother) and *caedere* (to kill).

9. **Populist**—A: A rural progressive desiring greater government action. From a small farmers' movement in 1892. Latin *populus* (of the people).

10. **mandate**—B: Authoritative order; expressed will of voters. When we give someone a *mandate* to clean up corruption, we symbolically place the problem in his hands. Latin *mandare* (to commit to one's charge).

11. **consensus**—A: General agreement; as, the *consensus* of party professionals. Unchanged from the Latin.

12. **disavow**—A: To repudiate; refuse to claim responsibility for; as, "He *disavowed* his plan to cut federal spending." Old French *desavotter*.

13. **gerrymander**—A: To alter a voting district unfairly. From Elbridge Gerry, governor of Massachusetts, whose party in 1812 changed a district's lines in Essex County. (Its changed shape resembled a *salamander*.)

14. **demagogue**—D: Political agitator; one who plays on emotions and prejudices to gain power. Greek *dēmagōgos* (leader of the people).

15. **telegenic**—B: Attractive on television; as, "It helps candidates to be *telegenic*." A new word from Greek *tēle* (far off) and *genic* (producing, born).

16. **bloc**—A: Group; combination of persons, parties or nations united for a common purpose; as, mobilizing the communist *bloc*. French *bloc* (block, lump, the whole lot).

17. **polarization**—C: A gathering of people around opposing viewpoints; as, the *polarization* of the community over busing. From positive and negative charges around opposite *poles* in an electric field.

18. **junket**—B: Travel; disparaging term referring to a government official's trip at public expense. Italian *giuncata* (a cream cheese).

19. **pork barrel**—D: Government funds used to ingratiate Congressmen with their constituents; as, "The Rivers-and-Harbors Bill is a *pork barrel* that has developed hundreds of projects." A colloquial farm term.
20. **radical**—A: One who holds extreme views and advocates far-reaching reforms. Latin *radicalis* (deeply rooted).

VOCABULARY RATINGS

20—18 correct ....exceptional
17—15 correct ....excellent
14—12 correct .... good

There Is Magic in a Word of Praise

BY FULTON OURSLER

A Broadway comedian once had an excruciating nightmare: he dreamed he was telling stories and singing songs in a crowded theater, with thousands of people watching him—but no one laughed or clapped.

"Even at $100,000 a week," he says, "that would be hell on earth."

It is not only the actor who needs applause. Without praise and encouragement anyone can lose self-confidence. Thus we all have a double necessity: to be commended and to know *how* to commend.

There is a technique in giving a compliment, a right way to go about it. It is no real compliment, for instance, to praise a man for some obvious attainment. Use discernment and originality. "That was a wonderfully convincing speech you made tonight," a gracious woman once said to a businessman. "I could not help thinking what a fine lawyer you would have made." The merchant flushed like a schoolboy at the *unexpected* character of the tribute. As André Maurois once remarked: "The general did not thank me when I talked to him of his victories, but his gratitude was unbounded when a lady mentioned the twinkle in his eye."

No one, great or obscure, is untouched by genuine appreciation. Yale's renowned English professor, William Lyon Phelps, related: "One hot summer day I went into a crowded railroad dining car for lunch. When the steward handed me the menu, I said, 'The boys in the kitchen certainly must be suffering today!' The steward looked at me in surprise. 'People come in here and complain about the food, kick about the service and growl about the heat. In 19 years you are the first person who has ever expressed any sympathy for the cooks back there in the kitchen.' What people want," Phelps concluded, "is a little attention as human beings."

In that attention, sincerity is essential. For it is sincerity that gives potency to a compliment. The man coming home after a hard day's work who sees the faces of his children pressed against the windowpane, waiting and watching for him, may water his soul with their silent but golden opinion.

The simple principles of the art of praise—to realize the human need for it, to compliment sincerely, and to train ourselves to look for the praiseworthy—help rub off the sharp edges of daily contact. And nowhere is this more true than in marriage. The wife or husband who is alert to say the heartening thing at the right moment has taken out valuable marriage insurance.

Women seem to have an instinct for such things; they look at life, so to speak, through their hearts. After his marriage, on February 23, a bridegroom remarked, "I will never forget our wedding anniversary. It will always be the day after Washington's birthday." "And I," his bride answered, "will never forget Washington's birthday. It will always be the day before we were married."

Children especially are hungry for reassurance, and the want of kindly appreciation in childhood can endanger the growth of character; it can even be a lifetime calamity. A young mother told the Rev. A. W. Beaven of a heartaching incident:

"My little daughter often misbehaves and I have to rebuke her. But one day she had been an especially good girl, hadn't done a single thing that called for reprimand. That night, after I tucked her in bed and started downstairs, I heard her sobbing. Turning back, I found her head buried in the pillow. Between sobs she asked, 'Haven't I been a *pretty* good girl today?'

"That question," said the mother, "went through me like a knife. I had been quick to correct her when she did wrong, but when she had tried to behave I had not noticed it. I had put her to bed without one word of appreciation."

The same principle—using the kind word—is potent in all human relationships. In my boyhood in Baltimore, a new drugstore opened in the neighborhood, and old Pyke Barlow, our skilled and long-established pharmacist, was outraged. He accused his young rival of selling cheap drugs and of inexperience in compounding prescriptions. Finally the injured newcomer, contemplating a suit for slander, went to see a wise lawyer, Thomas G. Hays. "Don't make an issue of it," Hays advised. "Try kindness."

Next day, when customers reported his rival's attacks, the new druggist said there must be a mistake somewhere. "Pyke Barlow," he told them, "is one of the finest pharmacists in this town. He'll mix emergency prescriptions any hour, day or night, and the care he takes with them sets an example for all of us. This neighborhood has grown— there's plenty of room for both of us. I'm taking Doc's store as the pattern for mine."

When the older man heard these remarks—because compliments fly on the winds of gossip quite as fast as scandal— he could not wait to meet the young fellow face to face and give him some helpful advice. The feud had been wiped out by sincere and truthful praise.

Wherever human beings gather, thoughtfulness is needed. In a group conversation the kind person will help everyone to feel a part of the discussion. A friend once paid this tribute to Prime Minister Arthur James Balfour as a dinner host: "He would take the hesitating remark of a shy man and discover in it unexpected possibilities, would expand it until its author felt he had really made some contribution to human wisdom. Guests would leave walking on air, convinced that they were bigger men than they had thought."

Why do most of us leave unuttered some pleasant truths that would make others happy? It would help if we remembered more often that "a rose to the living is more than sumptuous wreaths to the dead." A charming old gentleman used to drop in at an antique shop near Conway, N. H., to sell merchandise. One day after he left, the antique dealer's wife said she wished they had told him how much they enjoyed his visits. The husband replied, "Next time let's tell him."

The following summer a young woman came in and introduced herself as the daughter of the salesman. Her father, she said, had died. Then the wife told her of the conversation she and her husband had had after her father's last visit. The visitor's eyes filled with tears. "How much good that would have done my father!" she exclaimed. "He was a man who needed reassurance."

"Since that day," says the shopowner, "whenever I think something nice about a person, I tell him. I might never have another chance."

As artists find joy in giving beauty to others, so anyone who masters the art of praising will find it blesses the giver as much as the receiver. It brings warmth and pleasure into commonplaces and turns the noisy rattle of the world into music.

Something good can be said about everyone. We have only to say it.

One Man's Mede

A master of words puts the English language through some
punishing exercises

BY CLIFTON FADIMAN

There is something to be said against puns. They upset the
dignity of speech, cut the ground of logic from under us.
We groan not only to convey disapproval but to cover dis-
comfiture.

To a great practitioner a pun is language on vacation,
but to the nonpractitioner it may seem more like language
in agony. The candid lover of puns will admit this charge.
He will cheerfully confess to a *preference* for language
under stress, as Dali prefers a melted watch to the correct
time.

Let us take a few test cases: In *Animal Crackers,* Groucho
Marx recalled that when shooting elephants in Africa he
found the tusks very difficult to remove—adding, however,
that in Alabama the Tuscaloosa. To the contrapuntalist such
a statement is quite irrelephant; to the propunent it is pleasing because it shows what language can produce under
pressure, in this case language showing both marks of strain
and the strain of Marx.

I will give you another. Once, on a television show, George S. Kaufman got himself mired in the word *euphemism*. After playing with it for a few seconds he turned to his fellow panelist Sam Levenson, declared, "Euphemism and I'm for youse'm," and closed the discussion. Now this, like Tuscaloosa, was pure purposeless play, art for art's sake, like doodling, whittling, singing in the bath. Mr. Kaufman of course is no less a master of the meaningful pun. One remembers his anguished cry at the poker table: "I'm being trey-deuced!" Among the greatest wordplays of all time is his unsettling remark that what is one man's Mede is another man's Persian.

Impromptu Puns, though not generally the finest, often supply the purest pleasure. Once when I was emceeing the quiz show *Information Please,* the experts were required to identify a certain Middle Eastern potentate. John Gunther confidently supplied the correct answer. "Are you Shah?" I ventured. "Sultanly," he replied. Such Impromptus are successful for the unrecapturable moment only; you cannot judge them in cold blood any more than you can grade fragrances by memory.

The simplest pun is based on the reuse of a word with a slight shift in meaning: S. J. Perelman's "Doctor, I've got Bright's disease and he's got mine." Or take Sydney Smith's famous remark. Observing two housewives screaming at each other across a courtyard, he remarked that they would never agree because they were arguing from different premises.

Slightly more complicated is the homonym. Here the words match in sound but not meaning. When the homonym is imperfect a certain wild touch of imagination is often present. Like: "The audience strummed their catarrhs" (Alexander Woollcott) or "The things my wife buys at auction are keeping me baroque" (Peter De Vries).

So far, we have been considering only single puns, depending on one word. We approach structural complication when we get to double puns. Here is a well-constructed one from S. J. Perelman's movie, *Horse Feathers*. The secretary, who has been holding a caller at bay in the anteroom, warns Groucho, "Jennings is waxing wroth," to which

Groucho replies, "Never mind. Tell Roth to wax Jennings for a while."

When the homonyms require a double take from the listener they acquire some of the uncanny charm of echoes. Here is a first-rate doublet of this sort by Franklin P. Adams: "Take care of your peonies and the dahlias will take care of themselves."

Polar to the Impromptu Pun is the Set-up or Circumstantial Pun. It is a blend of narrative and wordplay, based on an imaginary, contrived situation, and it may be polished till it gleams. I offer a classic by Bennett Cerf.

It seems that a relative and namesake of Syngman Rhee, visiting our country to learn the magazine business, got a job on *Life*. On his first assignment, however, he lost himself in the mazes of New York City. It took several days to track him down. At last the Missing Persons Bureau investigator found him in a Third Avenue bar and cried in relief, "Ah, sweet Mr. Rhee, of *Life*, at last I've found you!"

A mere half-century ago the ability to pun via Latin was common, if not compulsory, among the well-educated. There is the reputed instance of Sir Charles James Napier's message to the British War Office after his capture of Sind in India. He is supposed to have telegraphed one word—*peccavi*—which, as the class knows, is Latin for "I have sinned."

To enjoy any art properly we learn to discriminate, inclining neither to wholesale rejection nor to uncritical acceptance. If we learn to avoid the mechanical, and to appreciate the genuinely good, then I think we may agree with James Boswell that, "a good pun may be admitted among the small excellencies of lively conversation."

Word Power Test No. 18

The Lore of Bench and Bar

BY PETER FUNK

In this list of verbs heard frequently in courts of law, check the word or phrase you believe is *nearest in meaning* to the key word. Answers are at the end of this test.

1. **militate** (mil′ ĭ tāt)—A: to make less severe. B: challenge. C: have weight or influence. D: arbitrate.

2. **extol** (eks tōl′)—A: to flatter. B: acknowledge. C: deprive of. D: praise.

3. **substantiate** (sub stan′ shĭ āt)—A: to confirm. B: indicate. C: substitute. D: emphasize.

4. **badger** (baj′ er)—A: to beat. B: pester. C: dig into. D: exhaust.

5. **cavil** (kav′ il)—A: to find fault. B: ridicule. C: dissemble. D: humble oneself.

6. **subvert** (sub vert′)—A: to replace. B: divide. C: sink. D: overthrow.

7. **jeopardize** (jep′ er dīz)—A: to unbalance. B: wear away. C: endanger. D: belittle.

8. **commandeer** (kom an dēr′)—A: to commit. B: take possession of. C: destroy. D: redirect.

9. **exhort** (eg zort′)—A: to urge. B: try hard. C: tamper with. D: shake down.

10. **mollify** (mol′ ĭ fī)—A: to deny. B: change. C: pacify. D: subdue.

11. **brandish** (bran′ dish)—A: to burn into. B: browbeat. C: torment. D: wave threateningly.

12. **incriminate** (in krim′ ĭ nāt)—A: to resist authority. B: accuse. C: imprison. D: rebuke.

13. **confound** (kon found′)—A: to perplex. B: probe deeply. C: frustrate. D: split up.
14. **nullify** (nul′ ĭ fī)—A: to retract. B: make ineffective. C: eliminate. D: numb.
15. **ingest** (in jest′)—A: to joke. B: disgorge. C: absorb. D: force in.
16. **evade** (e vād′)—A: to rub out. B: lurch. C: glance off. D: avoid.
17. **ravage** (rav′ ij)—A: to rage. B: devastate. C: take by storm. D: torture.
18. **lacerate** (las′ er āt)—A: to nurse. B: scold. C: bruise. D: tear.
19. **contend** (kon tend′)—A: to struggle. B: face boldly. C: plead. D: demand.
20. **prevaricate** (pre var′ ĭ kāt)—A: to put off. B: quibble. C: lie. D: forestall.

ANSWERS

1. **militate**—C: To have weight, influence or effect; as, circumstances that *militate* against a fair trial. Latin *militare* (to serve as a soldier).
2. **extol**—D: To praise lavishly; glorify; eulogize; as, to *extol* the character of the accused. Latin *extollere* (to lift up).
3. **substantiate**—A: To confirm; establish by proof or evidence; verify; as, to *substantiate* one's claim of innocence. Latin *substare* (to stand firm).
4. **badger**—B: To pester; harass or annoy persistently; bait; as, to *badger* a witness. From the once popular sport of harassing *badgers* with dogs.
5. **cavil**—A: To find trivial faults with; raise frivolous or picayune objections to; carp; as, to *cavil* at an investigator's methods. Latin *cavillari*.
6. **subvert**—D: To overthrow from the foundation; ruin; corrupt by undermining morals, allegiance or faith; as, a plot to *subvert* the government. Latin *subvertere* (to turn from beneath).
7. **jeopardize**—C: To endanger; imperil; expose to loss, injury or risk; as, to *jeopardize* one's career. Old French *jeu parti* (divided game).
8. **commandeer**—B: To take forcible possession of; seize for

public or military necessity; as, to *commandeer* a citizen's car. Old French *comander*.

9. **exhort**—A: To urge or advise earnestly; spur on; incite; as, to *exhort* a jury to show compassion. Latin *exhortari* (to encourage).

10. **mollify**—C: To pacify; soothe; soften the temper of; as, to *mollify* an angry crowd. Latin *mollificare*, from *mollis* (soft).

11. **brandish**—D: To wave or shake threateningly; flourish menacingly; as, to *brandish* a gun. Old French *brand* (sword).

12. **incriminate**—B: To accuse of or connect with a crime; implicate; as, to *incriminate* a suspect. Latin *incriminare*, from *crimen* (crime).

13. **confound**—A: To perplex; bewilder; mix up; as, to *confound* people with legal double-talk. Latin *confundere* (to pour together, confuse).

14. **nullify**—B: To make ineffective, useless or valueless; annul; as, to *nullify* a contract. Latin *nullificare*, from *nullus* (none).

15. **ingest**—C: To absorb; take in for digestion, as food into the stomach; as, to *ingest* relevant facts. Latin *ingerere* (to carry in).

16. **evade**—D: To avoid; turn aside; avert; as, to *evade* a crucial question. Latin *evadere* (to get off, escape).

17. **ravage**—B: To devastate; lay waste; plunder; as, a face *ravaged* by grief. Middle French *ravir* (to ravish).

18. **lacerate**—D: To tear or rend roughly; mangle; as, to *lacerate* the skin; also, to cause acute mental pain to; distress. Latin *lacerare* (to tear).

19. **contend**—A: To struggle; strive or vie in competition, or against difficulties or obstacles; as, to *contend* with prejudice. Latin *contendere* (to strain, exert).

20. **prevaricate**—C: To lie; stray from the truth; speak equivocally; as, to *prevaricate* under cross-examination. Latin *praevaricari* (to walk crookedly).

VOCABULARY RATINGS

20—18 correct ....exceptional
17—15 correct ....excellent
14—12 correct .... good

Watch Your Language!

BY THEODORE M. BERNSTEIN

How well do you use words? When you talk, write a letter or compose a memo to the boss, do you say what you mean? If you think you do, look at the following common errors culled from the pages of the New York Times.

ADVANCE PLANNING. "With a little advance planning, culinary chores for Easter can be simplified." Planning is the laying out of a future course; "advance" is therefore superfluous.

ANOTHER. "New York's public schools will greet their 890,700 boys and girls today . . . another 331,000 will attend the parochial schools." "Another" means "one more of the same kind." Thus "another" would be correct here only if the second figure were the same as the first figure. Why not use "more"?

AS THE CROW FLIES. "Karachi, Pakistan, is 2300 miles from Ankara, Turkey, as the crow flies." This once shiny figure of speech antedates aviation days and is mighty tarnished now. Why not "by air"?

BRING TO A HEAD. "The matter was brought to a head last Monday." This is not only a cliché but a repulsive one. To bring to a head means to suppurate, or cause pus to form.

BY MEANS OF. "The spindle is rotated by means of a foot pedal." Generally, "by" will serve nicely for "by means of."

CENTER. "The strikers' grievances center around vacation provisions." The verb "center" means "to be collected or gathered to a point." Therefore, use "center on" or "center in," but not "center around."

CHAIN REACTION. "Jackie Gleason's unrehearsed fall set off a chain reaction of thousands of local and long-distance telephone calls." "Chain reaction" does not mean a great quantity; it means a process in which a cause produces an effect that in turn becomes a cause, and so on.

CLAIM. "Mr. Casper claimed that a college degree was a business necessity." "Claim" should not be used as a synonym for "say," "assert" or "declare" except when there is at issue an assertion of a right or title.

COLLISION. "Mr. Crotty was changing a tire when a second car smashed into his automobile. The collision ruptured the gasoline tank." When two things collide, they strike against each other; both are in motion. No collision here; it was the "crash" or the "impact."

COMPRISE. "He gave the names of four books that comprised the body of Roman civil law." "Comprise" means "contain, embrace, include, comprehend." Thus, the whole comprises the parts, but not vice versa. What is wanted here is "compose," "constitute" or "make up."

CONTINUALLY. "When McSorley's finally closes its swinging doors, the oldest place in town that has been continually in the business will be Pete's Tavern." The word here should be "continuously." "Continual" means over and over again; "continuous" means unbroken.

DILEMMA. "The question is basically the common suburban dilemma: Should construction of apartments be allowed in former one-family areas?" A dilemma is a situation entailing a choice between two distasteful alternatives. There was no suggestion here of such alternatives. Use "problem" or "predicament."

FLAUNT. "Secretary Dulles charged the South Korean government with 'unilateral action' flaunting the authority of the United Nations command." "Flaunt" means to wave or to make a boastful display. "Flout," which the writer had in mind but couldn't quite reach, means to treat with contempt.

FORTUITOUS. "So Tobin wound up with the Lions, who already had an ace quarterback in Bobby Layne. Never was a more fortuitous deal made." "Fortuitous" means "happening by chance"; it does not mean fortunate.

FOUNDER. "The schooner foundered and apparently sank in heavy seas." If it foundered, it sank—because that's what "foundered" means. The word has a built-in sink.

INFER. "Was I attempting to belittle a great American writer when I inferred that *Moby Dick* is overstuffed?" To infer is to deduce; to imply (which is here the intended meaning) is to signify or to hint.

IN ORDER. "The United States and France have invited Yugoslavia to send a military mission to Washington in order to discuss defensive planning." Delete "in order," unless you are being paid by the word.

INTRIGUE. "He has always been intrigued by big problems." This use is best avoided on at least two grounds. First, it is an erroneous borrowing from French, in which the word means "puzzle"; second, "intrigue" has become a kind of fuzzy, all-purpose word to express meanings for which there are already perfectly good, precise words like "interest," "pique" and "excite."

LESS. "He could get even less games than did Hoad." The general rule is to use "less" for amount and "fewer" for number.

LIVID. "Provoo's face became livid. He leaned forward, banged his fist on the witness box and shouted." "Livid" means either black-and-blue or the color of lead. It does not mean vivid or red.

MASTERFUL. "In a masterful display of seamanship . . ." The distinction in good current usage between "masterful" (imperious, domineering) and "masterly" (skillful, expert) is worth preserving.

PINCH HITTER. As a synonym for "substitute" or "replacement," the phrase is a weary cliché. In addition, it usually is misused. In baseball, of course, a pinch hitter is a player sent to bat because his manager believes he will do a better job in the circumstances than the man he is replacing. A tenor hastily inserted in the cast to replace a singer who is indisposed is not a "pinch-hitting tenor." He is not expected to do as good a job as the missing star, much less a better one.

PREPARATORY. "As the former Far Eastern commander reviewed his service in the Orient preparatory to leaving for Paris . . ." The review in no sense prepared him for his departure; what the writer meant was simply "before."

RAVISHING. "Elm Beetle Infestation Ravishing Thousands of Trees in Greenwich." Insex? Keep your mind on your work. The word you want is "ravaging."

REASON . . . BECAUSE. "He said the reason he had broken down was because his mother had died two days before the hearing." "Reason" and "because" have the same connotation. Eliminate one or the other.

TRUE FACTS. "No matter what the true facts of the situation are . . ." Delete "true"; there are no such things as false facts.

-WISE. "Saleswise, the new candies are doing well." Slapping the suffix "-wise" onto words promiscuously and needlessly is, at the moment, a fad. Help stamp it out.

My, O Myopia!

BY CORNELIA OTIS SKINNER

Long running in New York City was a highly successful musical called *Applause*. The only fault I could find with this smash hit was its title, which was to be seen all over town. I invariably read it as *Applesauce*.

All my life I've been prone to read words incorrectly. As a girl, I commuted weekly by train to a nearby town for piano lessons. At either end of the day coach was a large printed notice which I deciphered as "Spitting Is Awful." Years passed before I discovered the rightful reading of this admonition.

My newspaper misreading usually occurs in the early morning when, bleary of eye and mind, I scan the headlines. Thus, some years ago, while sipping coffee, I read, "Demons to Convene in Indianapolis"—which produced a momentary wobble of my cup. I could see swarms of these creatures milling about a hotel lobby in their traditional red costumes, lining up for their name badges at tables presided over by smiling, satanic ladies. Halfway through this daydream, I glanced again at the headline to realize that the forthcoming convention would be made up merely of "Demos"—a space-saving typesetter having eliminated the "crat."

Once, on a plane trip, I was reading a magazine article by Pearl Buck. In a moment, one of those enchanted sentences caught my eye. It went: "At dawn we set forth in sedan chairs whose poles rested on the shoulders of bare-backed Chinese beavers." How extraordinary! I thought. The Chinese beaver must be a good deal larger than ours, and is obviously capable of being domesticated. At that point, the plane went into one of those inexplicable shudders, which jolted me into losing my place. When I found it again, I realized that Mrs. Buck and her party had been carried by Chinese *bearers*.

This tendency to transform words into something that they are not would undoubtedly be of significance to a psychiatrist, but I don't want to be told what it implies. Besides, I sometimes find the errors rather diverting. One day on a New York bus around Eastertime, I read in an overhead ad: "All our food is personally supervised by rabbits." Now, really! I thought. What won't the Madison Avenue boys resort to next? I imagined the Easter Bunny supervising the making of huge batches of chocolate eggs. Glancing again, I saw instead a Star of David and the kosher-market ad announcing that all its food was "personally supervised by *rabbis*." This, of course, was as it should be—but I still think the mental picture of a rabbit presiding over a candy kitchen is more colorful.

I might resort to the pretext that the majority of the words I misread are in small print, and that my eyesight is not what it was. However, I make the same mistakes in boldface newspaper advertisements. Last winter, a sports shop announced in oversized letters that it was CALLING ALL SKIERS TO ATTEND OUR GIANT SALE ON TERMINAL UNDERWEAR. The ad, with its ominous note of impending disaster, started me thinking about all those intrepid winter-sports enthusiasts arising in the dark of a frigid morning and deliberately getting into their terminal underwear prior to venturing forth to the snowcapped heights. Their we-who-are-about-to-die frame of mind, while courageous, struck me as incomprehensible. Even the subsequent discovery that their under-wear is *thermal* hasn't dissuaded me from the opinion that most skiers are crazy.

It is a comfort to run across others who have similar reading failings. For example, a dear friend of mine who is a crossword-puzzle fiend phoned me not long ago, saying, "You spend a lot of time in London. What is the district in which they drink illy-gally?"

"Drink what?" I asked.

"Illy-gally," she answered. "You know, it's one of those whimsical British names like shandygaff or cockaleekie."

I asked her how it was used. She replied in the tones of one addressing a backward child. "It simply says, 'District in London where one may drink illy-gally.'"

"How do you spell illy-gally?" I persisted.

"Why, i-l-l . . ." There was a pause, in which she said, "Oh . . ." Then she went on: "e-g-a-l-l-y."

I said nothing.

"You see," she continued quite crossly, "the word came at the end of a line, and if you ask me that's no way to hyphenate a harmless little word like 'illegally.'"

I'm rather sorry there is no such drink as illy-gally. I was beginning to enjoy the prospect of my next visit to London. I am sorry, too, that a convention of demons was never held in Indianapolis. If these visual delusions are abnormal, they at least give way to fantasies which are sometimes more entertaining than the actual printed words. That is why I would never dream of going in for any course in remedial reading.

Word Power Test No. 19

High School Specials

BY PETER FUNK

The words in the following list appear frequently in tests given to high-school students. Check the word or phrase you believe is *nearest in meaning* to the key word. Answers appear at the end of this test.

1. **indignity** (in dig′ nǐ tē)—A: penalty. B: humiliation. C: blame. D: rebuke.

2. **abstract** (ab strakt′; ab′-)—A: theoretical. B: confused. C: indefinite. D: unrealistic.

3. **brackish** (brăk′ ish)—A: backward. B: having a foul odor. C: salty. D: weedy.

4. **heyday** (hā′ dā)—A: excitement. B: special event. C: comedy. D: peak period.

5. **efface** (ě făs′)—A: to degrade. B: erase. C: mar. D: avoid

6. **cerebral** (sě rē′ bral)—A: formal. B: perceptive. C: impressionable. D: relating to the brain.

7. **solecism** (sŏl′ ě sěz′m)—A: plausible but fallacious argument. B: grammatical error. C: wise saying. D: comfort.

8. **nonentity** (non en′ tǐ tē)—A: trifle. B: mystical being. C: insignificant person. D: minor.

9. **succulent** (sŭk′ ū lent)—A: greedy. B: tasty. C: juicy. D: soft.

10. **musty** (mus′ tē)—A: moldy. B: gloomy. C: acrid. D: grubby.

11. **itinerant** (ī tin′ er ant)—A: irregular. B: temporary. C: poor. D: traveling.

12. **defray** (de frā′)—A: to pay. B: pull back. C: tatter. D: go around.
13. **medallion** (mĕ dal′ yun)—A: souvenir. B: precious metal. C: religious relic. D: large medal.
14. **duplicity** (dū plis′ ĭ tē)—A: repetition. B: artlessness. C: double-dealing. D: cleverness.
15. **caricature** (kăr′ ĭ ka tūr)—A: biographical sketch. B: cartoon likeness. C: eccentricity. D: personality trait.
16. **heinous** (hā′ nus)—A: abominable. B: obscure. C: treasonable. D: ugly.
18. **fettle** (fet′ ′l)—A: condition. B: shackle. C: humor. D: problem.
19. **lineage** (lin′ ē ij)—A: chain of command. B: prestige. C: ancestry. D: rigging.
20. **undue** (un dū′)—A: undisciplined. B: usurious. C: premature. D: unjustified.

ANSWERS

1. **indignity**—B: Humiliating treatment; offense against one's dignity or self-respect; outrage; as, to subject POWs to one *indignity* after another. Latin *indignus* (unworthy).
2. **abstract**—A: Theoretical; lacking specific factual instances; difficult to understand; abstruse; as, an *abstract* philosophical concept. Latin *abstrahere* (to draw away, withdraw).
3. **brackish**—C: Somewhat salty; unpleasant-tasting; not drinkable; as, *brackish* bay water. Dutch *brak* (salty).
4. **heyday**—D: Peak period; time of greatest strength, prosperity or success; as, the *heyday* of the whaling industry.
5. **efface**—B: To erase; obliterate; also, to withdraw (oneself) from attention; make (oneself) modestly inconspicuous; as, a shy child trying to *efface* herself in the group. Middle French *effacer*.
6. **cerebral**—D: Relating to the brain or the intellect; appealing to intellectual appreciation; as, *cerebral* discourses. Latin *cerebrum* (brain).
7. **solecism**—B: Grammatical error; minor blunder in speech; also, a breach of etiquette or decorum. Greek *soloikos* (speaking incorrectly).

8. **nonentity**—C: Insignificant person; one who is wholly un-distinguished in character, talents or achievement; as a po-litical *nonentity*. Latin *non-* (not), and *entitas* (being).

9. **succulent**—C: Juicy; full of freshness or richness; as, a *succulent* cut of meat. Latin *succulentus*, from *succus* (juice, sap).

10. **musty**—A: Moldy; smelling of dampness and decay; as, a *musty* cellar.

11. **itinerant**—D: Traveling from place to place; making a reg-ular or seasonal circuit; as, an *itinerant* fruit picker. Latin *itinerari* (to journey).

12. **defray**—A: To pay; provide for payment of; reimburse; as, to *defray* travel expenses. French *défrayer*.

13. **medallion**—D: Large medal; tablet or panel in a wall or window bearing a figure in relief, a portrait or an ornament; as, a commemorative *medallion*. French *médaillon*.

14. **duplicity**—C: Double-dealing; deliberate deception in speech or action belying one's true thoughts or intentions; as, to practice *duplicity*. Latin *duplex* (twofold, double).

15. **caricature**—B: Cartoon likeness achieved by exaggeration and often ludicrous distortion of a peculiar feature or char-acteristic; as, the art of *caricature*. Italian *caricare* (to load).

16. **heinous**—A: Abominable; extremely wicked; hateful or shockingly evil; as, a *heinous* murder. Middle French *hai-neus*, from *haine* (hate).

17. **emit**—B: To give off; send out; utter; as, to *emit* a roar. Latin *emittere* (to send out).

18. **fettle**—A: Condition; state of fitness, health, spirits; as, to be in fine *fettle*. Middle English *fetlen* (to shape, set in order).

19. **lineage**—C: Ancestry; line of descent or tradition; back-ground; origin; as, a custom of ancient *lineage*. Old French *ligne* (line of descent).

20. **undue**—D: Unjustified; immoderate; excessive; as, the *un-due* waste of natural resources. Middle English *undewe*.

VOCABULARY RATINGS

20—18 correct ....exceptional
17—15 correct ....excellent
14—12 correct .... good

"Englisch As She Is Goodly Spocken"*

BY NINO LO BELLO

Fractured English is the name of the game. It's fun to play, and all you have to do is travel with pad at the ready. Here is a sampling from my flip-of-the-tongue collection gathered abroad, beginning with an Italian doctor's sign: *Specialist in Women and Other Diseases*.

Even the British, who speak English themselves, muff one occasionally, as in this hospital sign in London: *Visitors. Two to a Bed and Half-an-Hour Only*. Or this linguistic lapse: *Our Establishment Serves Tea in a Bag Like Mother*.

One hotel in France lists an egg on its menu as *extract of fowl*. It can be ordered *peached or sunside up*.

Then there is the dentist in Istanbul whose doorway proclaims: *American Dentist, 2th Floor—Teeth Extracted By Latest Methodists*. At least he picked the right floor.

The problem extends to communist nations courting tourists. In Belgrade's state-owned skyscraper hotel, the Slavija, the elevator instructions say: *To move the cabin push*

*From a sign in the Netherlands advertising a Dutch-English grammar.

201

button of wishing floor. If the cabin should enter more persons, each one should press number of wishing floor. Posted in another Yugoslav hotel: *Let Us Know About Any Unficiency As Well As Leaking On The Service. Our Utmost Will Improve.*

I found this piece of prose in the office of one of Czechoslovakia's state travel bureaus: *Take One Of Our Horse-Driven City Tours—We Guarantee No Miscarriages.* And these lifesaving instructions aboard a Soviet ship in the Black Sea: *Help savering apparata in emergings behold many whistles! Associate the stringing apparata about the bosoms and meet behind. Flee then to the indifferent life-savering shippen obediencing the instructs of the vessel chef.*

On the elevator door in a Romanian hotel I found my all-time favorite: *The lift is being fixed for the next days. During that time we regret that you will be unbearable.*

Word Power Test No. 20

A Nosegay of Look-Alikes

BY PETER FUNK

In this list of paired words, similar enough in form to be confusing, check the word or phrase you believe is *nearest in meaning* to the key word. Answers appear at the end of this test.

1. **censor** (sen′ ser)—A: to scold. B: delete. C: fabricate. D: deceive.

2. **censure** (sen′ shure)—A: to reject. B: suppress. C: blame. D: remove from office.

3. **expatiate** (eks pā′ she āt)—A: to enlarge upon. B: reconcile. C: lavish. D: atone.

4. **expatriate** (eks pā′ tre āt)—A: to disqualify. B: enjoin. C: disown. D: exile.

5. **tortuous** (tor′ tū us)—A: slow. B: arduous. C: winding. D: cautious.

6. **torturous** (tor′ tūr us)—A: rough. B: morally irregular. C: sluggish. D: painful.

7. **presentiment** (pre zen′ tĭ ment)—A: composure. B: premonition. C: alarm. D: donation.

8. **presentment** (pre zent′ ment)—A: presentation. B: hunch. C: verdict. D: authorization.

9. **adverse** (ad vurs′)—A: dangerous. B: obstructive. C: upside down. D: unfavorable.

10. **averse** (a vurs′)—A: talkative. B: frustrating. C: unwilling. D: preventive.

11. **credible** (kred′ ĭ b'l)—A: believable. B: superstitious. C: gullible. D: skeptical.

12. **creditable** (kred′ it a b′l)—A: plausible. B: desirable. C: risky. D: praiseworthy.

13. **factious** (fak′ shus)—A: caustic. B: relating to a contentious group. C: manufactured. D: pointed.

14. **fractious** (frak′ shus)—A: unruly. B: splintered. C: crooked. D: frail.

15. **hypercritical** (hī per krit′ ĭ kal)—A: deceitful. B: over-critical. C: fearful. D: seriously ill.

16. **hypocritical** (hip o krit′ ĭ kal)—A: mistrustful. B: fussy. C: insincere. D: overly concerned with health.

17. **affect** (ă fekt′)—A: to influence. B: upset. C: emote. D: conclude.

18. **effect** (ĕ fekt′)—A: to modify. B: bring about. C: devise. D: regulate.

19. **presumptive** (pre zump′ tiv)—A: hopeful. B: insolent. C: probable. D: decisive.

20. **presumptuous** (pre zump′ tū us)—A: hasty. B: bombastic. C: inferred. D: arrogant.

ANSWERS

1. **censor**—B: To delete, alter or ban after official examination; as, to *censor* news. Latin *censere* (to assess).

2. **censure**—C: To blame; criticize; reprimand officially; as, to *censure* a legislator. Latin *censere*.

3. **expatiate**—A: To enlarge upon; elaborate; speak or write at length or in detail; as, in *expatiate* on the fuel problem. Latin *expatiari* (to digress).

4. **expatriate**—D: To exile; banish; also, to renounce allegiance to one's native land. Latin *expatriare* (to leave one's own country).

5. **tortuous**—C: Winding; full of twists and turns; as, a *tortuous* mountain trail; also, devious; as, *tortuous* reasoning. Latin *torquere* (to twist).

6. **torturous**—D: Cruelly painful; agonizing; causing torture; as, hours of *torturous* worry. Latin *torquere*.

7. **presentiment**—B: Premonition; foreboding; a feeling that something is about to happen. Latin *praesentire* (to perceive beforehand).

8.   **presentment**—A: • Presentation; a formal statement to an authority of a matter to be dealt with; as, a *presentment* returned by a grand jury on the subject of organized crime. Latin *praesentare* (to present).

9.   **adverse**—D: Unfavorable; opposed to one's interests; antagonistic; as, *adverse* criticism. Latin *advertere* (to turn toward).

10.   **averse**—C: Unwilling; reluctant; hesitant; as, to be *averse* to getting up early. Latin *avertere* (to turn away from).

11.   **credible**—A: Believable; entitled to confidence; trustworthy; as, a *credible* witness. Latin *credere* (to believe).

12.   **creditable**—D: Praiseworthy; deserving credit or esteem; as, a *creditable* performance. Latin *creditus*, "that which is believed," from *credere*.

13.   **factious**—B: Relating to or caused by a contentious group or groups; as, a political party split by *factious* disputes. Latin *factio* (faction).

14.   **fractious**—A: Unruly; hard to manage; refractory; as, a *fractious* horse. Latin *frangere* (to break).

15.   **hypercritical**—B: Overcritical; marked by excessive fault-finding; captious; as, a *hypercritical* book review. Greek *hyper-* (over), and *kritikos* (able to judge).

16.   **hypocritical**—C: insincere; relating to one who professes qualities or virtues he does not have. Greek *hypocritēs* (actor, pretender).

17.   **affect**—A: To influence; produce a noticeable reaction, response or change in; as, areas *affected* by the tornado. Latin *afficere* (to exert an influence).

18.   **effect**—B: To bring about; achieve; produce; as, to *effect* a cure. Latin *efficere* (to bring about).

19.   **presumptive**—C: Based on probability or presumption; supposed; providing grounds for reasonable opinion or belief; as, *presumptive* evidence. Latin *praesumere* (to anticipate, suppose, take for granted).

20.   **presumptuous**—D: Arrogant; unduly confident; overweening; taking liberties; as, a *presumptuous* manner. Latin *praesumere*.

VOCABULARY RATINGS

20—18 correct ....exceptional
17—15 correct ....excellent
14—12 correct .... good

The American Language

BY H.L. MENCKEN

The first Englishman to notice an Americanism sneered at it aloofly, thus setting a fashion that many of his countrymen have been following ever since. He was one Francis Moore, a ruffian who came to Georgia in 1735, and the word that upset him was *bluff*, in the sense of "a cliff or headland with a broad precipitous face." He did not deign to argue against it; he simply dismissed it as "barbarous," and for nearly a century, when it was printed at all in Great Britain, it was set off by sanitary quotation marks. But, in 1830, the eminent Sir Charles Lyell used it shamelessly and from that day to this it has been a respectable if somewhat unfamiliar word in England.

Its history is the history of almost countless other Americanisms. They have been edging their way into English since early colonial times, but only after running a gantlet of opposition. After the Revolution, that opposition took on the proportions of a holy war. Never an American book came out that the English reviewers did not belabor its vocabulary violently. Even serious writers like Jefferson, John Marshall, Noah Webster, and John Quincy Adams got their share. Jefferson's crime was that he had invented the verb *to belittle*. It was, one may argue plausibly, a very logical, useful, and perhaps even nifty word, and 75 years later the prissy Anthony Trollope was employing it without apology. But in 1787 *The London Review* roared: "What an expression! It may be an elegant one in Virginia, but all we can do is to *guess* at its meaning. For shame, Mr. Jefferson! Freely we forgive your attacks upon our national character; but for the future spare, we beseech you, our mother tongue!"

The underscoring of *guess* was a fling in passing at another foul Americanism. It was the belief of most Englishmen then, as it is today, that the use of the verb in the sense of *to suppose* or *assume* originated in this country. It is actually to be found, in that meaning precisely, in *Measure for Measure;* nay, in Chaucer. *To advocate* offers another example. It appeared in English in the dark backward and abysm of time, but during the 18th century it seems to have dropped out of general use. Toward the end of the century it came into vogue in this country, and soon made its way back to the land of its birth. It was received with all the honors proper to an invasion of Asiatic cholera, the reviews denouncing it as loutish, "Gothic," and against God.

The heroic struggle to keep Americanisms out of Britain still flourishes. A few years ago the Rt. Rev. Cyril Henry Gelding-Bird, Assistant Bishop of Guildford and Archdeacon of Dorking, was charged before the Farnham (Surrey) magistrates with applying *speed-cop* to a member of the *mobile police*. His Lordship denied with some heat that he had used the term, or anything else so unseemly, but the magistrates apparently concluded that he must have let it slip, for they took a serious view of his very modest adventure in speeding, fined him £10, and suspended his driving license for three months.

Whenever an Americanism comes publicly into question in England, there are efforts to track down its etymology, with results that are sometimes extremely bizarre. In January, 1935, for example, the London *Morning Post* opened its columns to a furious discussion of the verb-phrase, *to get his goat*. I content myself with one of the explanations: "Among the Negroes in Harlem it is the custom for each household to keep a goat to act as general scavenger. Occasionally one man will steal another's goat, and the household débris then accumulates to the general annoyance." The truth is that *to get his goat* seems to be of French origin, and in the form of *prendre sa chèvre*, has been traced back to the year 1585.

Occasionally, of course, genuine Americanisms are claimed as really English. In 1934 even the learned Dr. C. T. Onions, one of the editors of the great *Oxford Dictionary*, succumbed to the madness by offering to find in the dictionary any alleged Americanism that a reporter for the London *Evening News* could name. The reporter began discreetly with *fresh* (in the sense of *saucy*), *to figure* (in the sense of *to believe* or *conclude*), and *to grill* (in the sense of *to question*), and Dr. Onions duly found them all. But when the reporter proceeded to *rake-off*, the editor had to admit that the earliest example in the dictionary was from an American work, and when *boloney* and *nerts* were hurled at him he blew up with a bang.

In the modern Englishman there seems to be very little of that ecstasy in word-making which so prodigiously engrossed his Elizabethan forebears. Shakespeare alone probably put more new words into circulation than all the English writers since Carlyle, and they were much better ones. The ideal over there today is not picturesque and exhilarating utterance, but correct and reassuring utterance. At its best it shows excellent manners and even a kind of mellifluous elegance; indeed, the English, taking one with another, may be said to write much better than we do. But what they write is seldom animated by anything properly describable as bounce. It lacks novelty, variety, audacity.

Herein lies the fundamental reason for the introduction of so many Americanisms into British English. They are adopted in England simply because England has nothing so apt or pungent to offer in competition with them. His Lordship of Guildford did not apply *speed-cop* to the *mobile policeman* as a voluntary act of subversion; he let it slip for the single reason that it was an irresistibly apposite and satisfying term. And so with other Americanisms. Confronted by the same novelty, the Americans always manage to fetch up a name for it that not only describes it but also illuminates it, whereas the English, since the Elizabethan stimulant oozed out of them, have been content merely to catalogue it. There was a brilliant exemplification of the two approaches in the early days of railways. The English called the wedge-shaped fender that was put in front of the first locomotives a *plough*, which was almost exactly what it was, but the Americans gave it the bold and racy appellation of *cow-catcher*. For the casting which guides the wheels from one rail to another the English coined the depressingly obvious name of *crossing-plate;* the Americans, setting their imaginations free, called it a *frog*. The American *movie* is much better than the English *cinema;* so is *radio* than *wireless*, though it may be Latin, and *shock absorber* vastly better than *anti-bounce clip*, and *bouncer* than *chucker-out*, and *chain store* than *multiple shop*. Confronting the immensely American *rubberneck*, Dr. J. Y. T. Greig of Newcastle could only exclaim "one of the best words ever coined!" And in the face of *lounge lizard*, Horace Annesley Vachell fell silent like Sir Isaac Newton on the seashore, overwhelmed by the solemn grandeur of the linguistic universe.

One finds in current American all the characters and tendencies that marked the rich English of Shakespeare's time—an eager borrowing from other languages, a bold and often very ingenious use of metaphor, and a fine disdain of the barricades separating the parts of speech. We had already a large repertory of synonyms for *jail*, but when the word *hoosegow* precipitated itself from the Spanish *juzgado* somewhere along the Rio Grande it won quick currency. *Bummer*, coming in from the German, is now clipped to *bum*. *Buncombe*, borrowed by the English as *bunkum*, has bred *bunco* and *bunk* and *to debunk* at home.

There are constant complaints in the English newspapers about the appearance of lawless American novelties in the parliamentary debates, and in discourses from the sacred desk. They begin to show themselves also in *belles lettres*. They even pop up in the diatribes that revile them; the Englishman, conquered at last, can no longer protest against

Americanisms without using them. If only because of the greater weight of the population behind it, the American form of English seems destined to usurp the natural leadership of British English, and to determine the general course of the language hereafter. But its chief advantage in this struggle is the fact that its daring experiments lie in the grand tradition of English, and are signs of its incurable normalcy and abounding vigor.

Name-Changing
—It's the Custom!

Most people don't realize how common name-changing is in this country. To a French count who renounced his name and title, it's one of our overlooked freedoms.

BY TED MORGAN

When I became an American citizen in February 1977, I renounced my title (I was a count in France) and changed my name to Ted Morgan. Sanche de Gramont, my ancestral name, identified me by national origin and social class. I wanted to make my name rather than inherit it. Just as I was choosing my nationality, I wanted to choose my name.

Several years before, a friend of mine who is a whiz at anagrams had drawn up a list of 19 possible names from the nine letters in de Gramont. In addition to Ted Morgan, it included Tom Danger, Rod Magnet, Monte Drag, Mo Dragnet and R. D. Megaton. I felt that Ted Morgan was forthright and practical, a name telephone operators and desk clerks could hear without flinching. Morgan was someone you could lend your car to. He would return it with a full tank of gas. Dogs and small children liked him. Editors knew that if he was not always brilliant, at least he was on time. And so, Ted Morgan.

At the naturalization ceremony, 30 other applicants for citizenship also changed their names. This was not unusual. Indeed, most people don't realize how common name-changing is in this country. It's one of the overlooked freedoms.

In America, changing your name is part of the culture, going back to the Indians, who changed their totemic names according to accomplishment. A chief of the Blackfeet Piegan tribe, for instance, known as Spotted Elk, changed his name to Chief of the Bears after leading a successful war party. A change of name was like a promotion.

Sometimes the change was less formal. Early German settlers names, for example, were often casually anglicized on their arrival. The Rockefellers were originally Rockenfellers from the lower Rhine. Did Ezra Pound, Herbert Hoover and General Pershing know that their people were Pfunds, Hubers and Pfoershings? Does Walter Cronkite know that his ancestral name is Krankheit?

Sometimes the abrasion of everyday speech simply wore down odd names. The De La Noyes, Huguenots from Holland, became Delanos. Boncoeur became Bunker. General Custer was the descendant of a Hessian mercenary named Kuester. Lincoln may have come from a family of Linkhorns.

But just as often, the change was deliberate. Paul Revere's father changed his name from Apollos Rivoire "merely on account that the bumpkins pronounce it easier." The evangelist Billy Sunday translated his name from his German immigrant father's Sonntag.

Shaking off an ethnic encumbrance was one reason for a change of name, but not the only one. Here are a few more.

ACCIDENT. When Vice President Walter Mondale's family came here from Norway, their name was Mondal. A clerk at Ellis Island added an "e," and one in Minnesota filled out the name on some homesteading forms as Mondale. To avoid any difficulties proving ownership, the family adopted the changed version.

FLIGHT. In America, people disappear all the time. They are casualties of the success ethic, or have had an overdose of family life, or are suffering from an identity crisis. People say they are going to the corner store for cigarettes, and step out into another life. It's easy enough to change one's name.

RIDICULE. A classic example is that of George Philpott, who in 1888 petitioned for a change of surname. He explained that he had a "cumbersome and mirth-provoking name . . . which suggests to that punning portion of the common public, many and annoying calembours upon utensils more or less intimately connected with the household." His petition was granted.

MOVIE NAMES. The right name is part of the discovered-in-the-drugstore success story. Would Marilyn Monroe have made it as Norma Jean Baker? In the labyrinthine minds of Hollywood producers, she needed that extra lift, that booster rocket, and so joined the queens of alliteration.

IMPRESSIVE NAMES. One example of a name that works is Learned Hand—for a judge. Not only is the judicial solemnity built in, but it was his real name (Learned was his mother's family name). Sometimes a slight alteration is in order, however. Thomas W. Wilson dropped his first name to become Woodrow Wilson, and Hiram Ulysses Grant (nicknamed "Useless" as a boy) became Ulysses S. Grant.

The doctoral thesis on the correlation between name-changers and over-achievers has yet to be written. Would Fred Friendly have reached the CBS executive suite as Ferdinand Wachenheimer? Would Mike Nichols have charmed Broadway and Hollywood as Michael Igor Peschkowsky?

HISTORICAL ASSOCIATIONS. Sometimes history intervenes. During World War II, several Hitlers applied for name changes. But not Master Sergeant Paul Hitler who said, in effect, "Let the other guy change his!"

What if a man wanted to change his obscure name for one made famous by the patina of history and the glitter of wealth? This is what Harry H. Kabotchnik decided to do in 1923 when he petitioned the court of change it to Cabot. The illustrious New England Cabots filed suit to prevent him. The objection was overruled by the court on the ground that there was nothing in the law to prevent the adoption of a famous name. Kabotchnik was merely shortening his name. The Cabots should be flattered that their name had been chosen. They could now talk, not only to God and the Lowells, but to Kabotchnik.

In similar fashion, immigrant Abraham Bitle changed his name to Biddle—and I changed mine to Morgan. There was a $25 naturalization fee, with no extra charge for the name change. It was the bargain of the century. I had a new name and a new feeling of self.

There is a gravestone in Virginia's Shenandoah Valley that says: "Here lie the remains of John Lewis, who slew the Irish Lord, settled in Augusta County, located in the town of Staunton, and furnished five sons to fight the battle of the American Revolution." Not being able to claim any comparable achievements, I think I would want my gravestone to read: "Here lie the remains of Ted Morgan, who became an American."

Word Power Test No. 21

Words Ending in "ite"

BY WILFRED FUNK

Surprisingly few words ending in *ite* are nontechnical, useful to know and hence not worthy test words. Before you begin this test, write down definitions of those words you think you know. Then check the word or phrase you believe is *nearest in meaning* to the key word. Answers are at the end of the test.

1. **erudite** (ĕr′ ŏŏ dite *or* ĕr′ ū dite)—A: proud. B: secret. C: learned. D: courteous.
2. **contrite** (kon trite′ *or* kon′ trite)—A: narrow-minded. B: repentant. C: restricted or hemmed in. D: uncertain.
3. **requite** (re quite′)—A: to repay. B: complete. C: demand. D: need.
4. **mite** (mite)—A: precious stone. B: strength. C: a small object. D: probability.
5. **indite** (in dite′)—A: to introduce. B: charge with a crime. C: put into words or writing. D: insult.
6. **anchorite** (ang′ kuh rite)—A: a hermit. B: a hard type of stone. C: a cruel burden. D: a durable metal.
7. **cite** (site)—A: to memorize. B: point out with a finger. C: see clearly. D: quote.
8. **sprite** (sprite)—A: a small pole. B: an elf or spirit. C: good cheer. D: mischief.
9. **satellite** (sat′ ĕ lite)—A: a sparkling. B: a ruler. C: a gem. D: a servile attendant.
10. **tripartite** (try pahr′ tite)—A: shared by three parties. B: sharply disputed. C: widely separated. D: seriously attempted.
11. **respite** (res′ pit)—A: breath. B: ill will. C: fatigue. D: an interval of rest.

12. **trite** (trite)—A: impudent. B: clever. C: commonplace. D: brief.

13. **incite** (in site′)—A: to cut off. B: arouse or stir up. C: perceive the inner nature of a thing. D: commence.

14. **parasite** (par′ ă site)—A: a disease. B: a hanger-on. C: a loss of motion and feeling. D: an insect exterminator.

15. **elite** (ĕ leet′)—A: state of being worn out with age. B: speed. C: the best people. D: unwholesomeness.

16. **recondite** (rek′ un dite *or* re kon′ dite)—A: carefully surveyed. B: exhaustive. C: difficult to comprehend. D: of high character.

17. **rite** (rite)—A: a solemn ceremony. B: justice. C: straightness. D: a cleansing.

18. **apposite** (ap′ uh zit)—A: appropriate or fitting. B: highly unpleasant. C: on a higher level. D: self-assertion.

19. **ignite** (ig nite′)—A: to shun. B: set on fire. C: strengthen. D: anger.

20. **expedite** (ex′ pĕ dite)—A: to experiment. B: agree to. C: speed up. D: start out or begin.

ANSWERS

1. **erudite**—C: From the Latin *eruditus*, (learned); scholarly; as, "He was *erudite* in the arts, but totally impractical in business affairs."

2. **contrite**—B: Repentant; conscience-smitten; as, "He was pathetically *contrite* for having given offense." From the Latin *contritus* (bruised).

3. **requite**—A: To make return; to pay back as for a benefit or injury; to recompense; as, "The wicked *requite* evil with evil."

4. **mite**—C: A small object; small amount; as, "He gave a mere *mite* of his fortune to charity."

5. **indite**—C: To put into words or writing; to compose; as "to *indite* a letter or poem." The Latin *in* (in), and *dictare* (to declare).

6. **anchorite**—A: A religious recluse; a hermit. Originally from the Greek *anachorein*, meaning "to retire."

7. **cite**—D: To quote; to refer to specifically; to mention as an illustration; as, "Please *cite* one authority who will support your argument." The Latin *citare* (to summon).

8. **sprite**—B: An elf or spirit; as, "She seemed more like a fairy *sprite* than a human being." Originally from the Latin *spiritus* (breath).

9. **satellite**—D: A servile attendant; as, "The king was surrounded by fawning *satellites*." From the Latin *satelles* (an attendant).

10. **tripartite**—A: From the Latin *tripartitus* (divided into three parts). Hence, shared by three parties; as, "These nations negotiated a *tripartite* treaty."

11. **respite**—D: An interval of rest or of relief from suffering; as, "Sometimes there seems to be no *respite* from worry." The Latin *respectus* (a delay).

12. **trite**—C: From the Latin *tritus* (rubbed). Hence, worn out by continuous use; hackneyed; as, "He made a *trite* comment about the weather."

13. **incite**—B: From the Latin *incitare* (to arouse or stir up); to stimulate to action; as, "He tried to *incite* the people to rebel."

14. **parasite**—B: An organism living in or on another organism, and so, by extension, a person who lives lazily at another's expense; a hanger-on; as, "He was a *parasite* who lived on his brother's earnings." The Greek *parasitos* (eating at the table of another).

15. **elite**—C: A French loan word meaning the best people; the choicest part of a society or group; the pick; as, "He fought in an *elite* regiment."

16. **recondite**—C: We speak of *recondite* studies or writing when they are profound and not easy to understand. The Latin *reconditus* (profound).

17. **rite**—A: A solemn or religious ceremony performed in a prescribed manner; as, "The priest performed the last *rites*." The Latin *ritus* (religious custom).

18. **apposite**—A: From the Latin *appositus* (appropriate and fitting); relevant; suitable; as, "His remarks were most *apposite* and to the point."

19. **ignite**—B: To set on fire; to kindle; as, "A spark would *ignite* the dry forest." From the Latin *ignis* (fire).

20. **expedite**—C: To speed up a process; to hasten the progress of anything; as, "The quartermaster must *expedite* supplies." From the Latin *expeditus* (unimpeded).

VOCABULARY RATINGS

20—18 correct ....excellent
17—15 correct .... good
14—11 correct .... fair

Accuracy Is a Winner's Policy

BY EVAN HILL

The electrician wiring my new house worked swiftly and efficiently. But I asked him, "Couldn't you put those outlets in closer to the floor? Six inches down, perhaps, where they won't be so conspicuous?"

He shook his head. "No," he said, "it's the code—the electrical code. They've got to be this height."

"State law?" I asked.

He nodded. "Town, too."

Next day I made a few telephone calls. Our state building code did not specify anything about the height of outlets. Our little town did not even have a building code. What the electrician referred to must have been just a local contractor's custom.

What difference did it make, six inches up or down? Not much, perhaps. Still, the electrician had been inaccurate about a matter in which he should be expert, and so had undercut my trust in him. If he made an obvious error like that, that I could see, what might be hidden behind the walls where I couldn't check? And what about the accuracy of the bill?

Our safety and sense of well-being—our life, in fact—depend on the degree to which we can trust the accuracy of the people we deal with. For example: In July 1971, a jumbo 747 jet was damaged on takeoff in San Francisco. Fortunately, no one was killed, although there were serious injuries. Later, the pilot testified that the flight dispatcher had told him his runway was 9500 feet long. Which it *was;* however, mostly because of construction work, only 8400 feet were available. This led to a miscalculated takeoff speed and the accident. Investigators thus came down to the use of incorrect takeoff speed, resulting from a series of irregularities, tiny pieces of misinformation, or lack of information. Every day thousands of passengers stake their lives on the gamble that bits of information vital to their safety will be transmitted with absolute, scrupulous accuracy.

Rocket scientist Hans Gruene recalls an incident during the 1950s when he was working on the Redstone Rocket. During an investigation following the failure of a Redstone mission, an engineer discovered a mistake made unknowingly while he was working on the rocket, and immediately reported his findings to Wernher von Braun, the head of the project. Instead of the expected reprimand, von Braun rewarded him—because, he said, it was vital to know just what had gone wrong.

The degree of accuracy maintained in the space program is illustrated by a statement von Braun made several years ago: "The Saturn 5 has 5,600,000 parts. Even if we had a 99.9-percent reliability, there would still be 5600 defective parts. Yet the Apollo 4 mission flew a 'textbook' flight with only two anomalies occurring, demonstrating a reliability of 99.9999 percent. If an average automobile with 13,000 parts were to have the same reliability, it would have its first defective part in about 100 years."

Inaccurate or imprecise language can lead to diplomatic incidents, or, conceivably, even to war. The English diplomat Sir Harold Nicolson decried "the horrors of vagueness." He wrote, "The essential to good diplomacy is precision. The main enemy is imprecision."

The charge of the Light Brigade, that famous 19th-century disaster, has been attributed to vague and misunderstood orders. Lord Raglan's aide may have compounded the confusion when he transmitted the order to Lord Lucan and gestured vaguely as to which guns were to be attacked. As a result, the Light Brigade rode into the very center of the Russian army rather than against a redoubt where the Russians, in disarray, were removing their guns. Whatever the reason, of the 609 British cavalrymen who made the charge, only 198 returned.

In every endeavor, precision counts. During the Olympics in Munich in 1972, two American athletes were disqualified because their coach had inaccurately interpreted the timetable and did not schedule his men's arrival correctly.

When my Uncle George remarked that a man "kept a dull ax," that was about as severe a condemnation as he could muster. And he applied that phrase to others besides woodsmen. I thought of Uncle George's saying when I worked on a newspaper with a photographer who labeled a picture of the White Mountains of New Hampshire as the Canadian Rockies. We laughed when he said it was just an error. Some error—3000 miles. I suspected I'd have to check every picture identification, and I was right.

Accuracy can never be overdone. A magazine editor once asked me if I knew a certain famous man who needed help with his writing.

"Yes, I know him," I said. "But I'm not sure he knows me. I have visited with him at least six times, and each time he needs to be introduced to me."

The editor exchanged a look with a colleague. "We asked," he said, "because you had *told* us you knew him, but when we telephoned him, he said he'd never heard of you. Now we understand." And I got the assignment.

Few executives consider accuracy a special virtue—they just expect it. The makers of loose and exaggerated statements may seem to get more attention, but the habit of accuracy casts a long shadow ahead. Its users are trusted, relied on, and so become obvious candidates for responsibility. After all, if you have a choice between a guess man and a fact man, which do you trust?

Inaccuracy irritates all kinds of human relationships. The man at the party who doesn't introduce us accurately perhaps doesn't care very much about us. How many husband-wife tempers have been lost on a Sunday drive because the copilot said a vague "That way," instead of "Next left" or "Straight ahead"? But accuracy in all our dealings sweetens relationships, averts misunderstandings and helps keep the peace.

How can we develop the art of accuracy? Here are some pointers.

1. Facts: do your homework. We live in a time of the instant opinion, the prefab argument and the pseudo-statistic. For example, we all "know" that Catholics have more children per family than Protestants. Actually, in America, Baptists have the highest birth rate; the birth rate among Catholics is, in fact, only a negligible fraction higher than among Protestants. We all "know" that one divorce leads to another. The fact is that more than 95 percent of all persons divorced have been divorced only once and, typically, either marry again and stay married—or do not re-marry.

Facts are not always known or easy to interpret. But we must do our homework so we at least know what the facts are thought to be. Further, we must give proper weighting to *all* the relevant facts, not "picking our cases" and ignoring those that weaken our position.

2. Precision: develop the reference-book habit. Accuracy is not just a matter of facts; it is also correct spelling, punctuation, grammar, measurement, context, relevance—in a word, precision. I learned this from my first city editor, who taught me that a door is not a doorway; that "no injuries were reported" does not mean "there were no injuries"; that a man *charged* with burglary is not necessarily a burglar.

As Dr. Richard Asher told aspiring medical writers in the *Journal of the American Medical Association*, "Look up everything you quote. You may be certain there is a book called *Alice in Wonderland*, and that it mentions a 'Mad Hatter'; that there is another book called *Alice Through the Looking Glass;* that Sherlock Holmes said, 'Elementary, my dear Watson'; and that in the Bible story of Adam and Eve, an apple is mentioned. In all five cases you are wrong."*

Finding what is true is not always easy. *New York Times* correspondent C. L. Sulzberger reports that once he played cards with Dwight D. Eisenhower, Averell Harriman, Alfred Gruenther and Dan Kimball, U.S. Secretary of the Navy, while they discussed the memoirs of James Forrestal, first Secretary of Defense. They all had attended a meeting referred to in the book, and each agreed that Forrestal's account was wrong. "But when I asked what, then, was the true version, all promptly disagreed."

Similar situations occur all the time. And to discover the facts then requires that we carefully weigh conflicting evidence and build one observation on another. This takes discipline, as well as a healthy skepticism. The accurate person will more often withhold his judgment than hazard a wild guess. He is more willing than most to say, honestly, "I do not know."

At its best, accuracy is a painstaking, caring, patient and reasonable faculty of mind. And ultimately it is creative, too. For it not only looks up facts, it discovers them in the first place.

*The first book cited was originally *Alice's Adventures in Wonderland*. It refers only to the "Hatter," never to the "Mad Hatter." The other Alice book is *Through the Looking-Glass*. The Holmes passage runs: " 'Excellent,' said I; 'Elementary,' said he." Finally, Genesis mentions no apples.

Cracking the Real-Estate Code

As most people have learned to their dismay, real-estate language often needs translation. Here's a handy guide to what those alluring phrases really mean.

BY RICHARD LIPEZ

HOUSES—U.S.A.	HOUSES—U.S.A.
COLONIAL: built prior to the second Eisenhower Administration	LEISURE HOME: habitable during July and August
GRACIOUS COLONIAL: you can't afford it	RANCH: egg box wearing a cowboy hat
VICTORIAN: drafty	RAISED RANCH: ranch set on a slope

HOUSES—U.S.A.

CHALET: ranch set on a steep slope

OLDER HOME: lists disconcertingly to the southwest

COMFORTABLE: small

COZY: teeny-weeny

CUTE: itsy-bitsy

IMMACULATE: kitchen walls not as greasy as the pit floor at Ralph's Garage

PATIO: spot near back door where cement truck overturned

PIAZZA: porch

GLEAMING BATHROOM: bathroom

VANITY BATHROOM: bathroom with a table nailed to the wall

CARRIAGE HOUSE: garage leaning against '48 Dodge

CONVENIENT TO SHOPPING: bay window overlooks an A&P parking lot

$300 TO HEAT: $780 to heat

HOUSES—U.S.A.

FAMILY ROOM: basement with 100-watt light bulb

NEEDS SOME FIXING UP: leg of bathtub protruding through kitchen ceiling needs polishing

BROOK ON PROPERTY: goes through the cellar

DESIRABLE CORNER: corner

ENTRANCE FOYER: door

MANY EXTRAS: recent owners left behind rags, coat hangers, half a bottle of cough syrup

NICE NEIGHBORHOOD: and let's keep it that way!

ONLY 15 MINUTES FROM...: only 40 minutes from...

SEEING IS BELIEVING: seeing is believing

MAKE AN OFFER: say something amusing

Word Power
Test No. 22

The French All Around Us

BY PETER FUNK

The English language has been said to be French badly pronounced. This hyperbole carries a measure of truth. The invasion of Britain by William the Conqueror in 1066 caused French to become our language of government, law and the military. Once English-speakers got the habit of borrowing, the process never stopped. Even today, the word *détente* confirms that we are still making withdrawals from the great riches of French. English has taken all of the words in this test—and thousands of others—from the French. Check the word or phrase you believe is *nearest in meaning* to the key word. Answers are at the end of the test.

1. **clairvoyance** (klair voy′ ans)—A: suggestibility. B: clarity of mind. C: statement of fact. D: extraordinary insight.
2. **chalice** (chal′ is)—A: lightweight fabric. B: Swiss-style house. C: goblet. D: ornament.
3. **facile** (fas′ ĭl)—A: effortless. B: flexible. C: candid. D: spontaneous.
4. **embezzle** (em bez′ l)—A: to decorate. B: praise. C: muzzle. D: steal.
5. **lavish** (lav′ ish)—A: servile. B: sizable. C: excessively generous. D: widespread.
6. **mirage** (mĭ rahzh′)—A: unexplained event. B: artificial stimulus. C: conundrum. D: optical illusion.
7. **ogre** (ō′ gur)—A: bore. B: rumor. C: tool. D: monster.
8. **menagerie** (mĕ naj′ er ē)—A: side show. B: collection of wild animals. C: establishment. D: kennel.
9. **jostle** (jos′ l)—A: to tease. B: endanger. C: temporize. D: shove.
10. **fief** (fēf)—A: territory one controls. B: musical instrument. C: social blunder. D: stolen goods.
11. **jaunty** (jawn′ tē)—A: lighthearted. B: venerable. C: earnest. D: jocose.

12. **ragout** (ră gōō′)—A: a stew. B: dance. C: fabric. D: disturbance.

13. **cliché** (klē shá′)—A: hasp. B: trite saying. C: convenience. D: reverie.

14. **posture** (pos′ chur)—A: hypothesis. B: stance. C: belief. D: conceit.

15. **aplomb** (ă plom′)—A: poise. B: contentment. C: corpulence. D: pardon.

16. **memoir** (mem′ wahr)—A: a secret. B: revelation. C: reminiscence. D: reminder.

17. **posterity** (pos ter′ ĭ tē)—A: antiquity. B: future generations. C: rump. D: good fortune.

18. **bastion** (bass′ chun)—A: illegitimacy. B: insouciance. C: dungeon. D: stronghold.

19. **lampoon** (lam pōōn′)—A: mountain sheep. B: satire. C: spear. D: tableau.

20. **brusque** (brusk)—A: curt. B: vague. C: conciliatory. D: efficient.

ANSWERS

1. **clairvoyance**—D: Extraordinary insight; ability to "see" what is not normally within our perceptions; as, to possess a *clairvoyance* for spotting economic trends. French *clair* (clear) and *voyant* (seeing).

2. **chalice**—C: Goblet; cup used for Holy Communion wine. "The priest held up the silver *chalice*." Medieval French.

3. **facile**—A: Effortless; moving with ease; as, the *facile* fingers of a pianist; a *facile* wit. Old French.

4. **embezzle**—D: To steal money entrusted to one's care; as, "The treasurer *embezzled* thousands of dollars." Old French *embesillier, en* (an intensive) and *besillier* (to destroy).

5. **lavish**—C: Excessively generous in spending or giving; prodigal; as *lavish* gifts or *lavish* use of water. Medieval French *lavasse* (a downpour of rain) from *laver* (to wash).

6. **mirage**—D: Optical illusion involving reflection; as, the *mirage* of a lake in the desert where no water exists. French *mirer* (to look at).

7. **ogre**—D: Monster; brutal person; in fairy tales, a man-eating giant. French, possibly from Latin Orcus (god of death or hell).

8. **menagerie**—B: Collection of wild animals; as, a circus *menagerie*. Old French *ménage* (household).

9.   **jostle**—D: To shove roughly; push; as, to *jostle* someone in a line. From Old French *jouster* (a combat on horseback between two knights).

10.   **fief**—A: Territory or domain that one controls or dominates. "A century ago, the city of New York was Boss Tweed's personal *fief*." Old French *fief* (fee, feudal estate).

11.   **jaunty**—A: Lighthearted and carefree; having a stylish self-confidence. "The child gave the men a *jaunty* nod." French *gentil* (genteel, gentle).

12.   **ragout**—A: A well-seasoned meat-and-vegetable stew. Apparently, 17th-century Frenchmen believed a *ragout* could awaken jaded palates. French *ragoûter* (to revive the taste).

13.   **cliché**—B: Trite saying. From *clicher*, French term for a stereotype (printing plate to reproduce many copies). The expression "hit the nail on the head" is a *cliché*.

14.   **posture**—B: Stance; bearing; pose. "Who knows what Napoleonic *postures* our Presidents take in front of White House mirrors?"

15.   **aplomb**—A: Poise; self-assurance; self-confidence; as, to face a difficult situation with *aplomb*. From Old French *à plomb* (being perpendicular according to a plumb line).

16.   **memoir**—C: Reminiscence; a personal record; an intimate biography; as, Jack Valenti's *memoir* of Lyndon B. Johnson. French *mémoire*.

17.   **posterity**—B: The future or succeeding generations; progeny. ". . . and secure the Blessings of Liberty to ourselves and our *Posterity* . . ." Medieval French *postérité*.

18.   **bastion**—D: Stronghold; any well-defended position. "Chicago, a *bastion* of Teamster strength." Old French *bastille* (fortress).

19.   **lampoon**—B: Satire. A 17th-century French drinking song—*lampons* (let us drink)—during which ribald jokes were composed; hence a ridiculing; as, Daumier's pictures *lampooning* lawyers.

20.   **brusque**—A: Curt; abrupt in manner and speech; as, the guard's *brusque* reply. French, from Italian *brusco* (sour-tasting).

VOCABULARY RATINGS

20—18 correct ....exceptional
17—15 correct ....excellent
14—12 correct .... good

"Everything Begins With a Pencil"

BY JEROME BRONDFIELD

We use them to do sums, prepare marketing lists, leave phone messages, record errant golf scores—or just to doodle with. We casually swipe them off other people's desks, stir drinks with them, prop up plants with them, print advertising and political slogans on them. We lose, discard or simply sharpen them away at a profligate rate. Some 2.5 *billion* of them (enough to circle the world 11 times at the equator) are manufactured and sold annually in the United States alone.

But you get the idea, right? There has just never been anything as downright *useful* as the plain old pencil. If you doubt it, think what the world was like without the modern pencil, which has been with us less than two centuries. The ancients—those few who mastered their cultures' writing forms—used exquisitely tiny brushes or reeds dipped in crude inks. (The Romans called their brush *penicillus*, or "little tail," from which comes "pencil.") The goose-quill pen was introduced in Europe in the sixth century.

A millennium rolled by. Then, in 1564, a violent storm blew down a large tree near Borrowdale in Cumberland, England. A mass of black, mineral-like substance was exposed where the tree's huge roots had been: a mother lode of plumbago, or "black lead." It was, simply, the purest graphite ever uncovered in Britain.

Local shepherds used pieces of the stuff to brand their sheep. But before long, sharp townsmen were cutting it into sticks and hawking them on London streets as "marking stones," for tradesmen and merchants to use on their crates and baskets. Then, in the 18th century, King George II seized the mine in Borrowdale and began operating it as a Crown monopoly. (Graphite, it seems, was indispensable in the precision shaping of cannon balls.) So zealous was the Crown in protecting its goodies that Parliament made it a hanging offense to poach graphite from the mine or its peripheral deposits in the surrounding countryside. The mine was worked only a few months a year to keep supply down and price up, and laborers were searched before leaving the mine shaft.

Early graphite marking sticks had two glaring deficiencies. They stained the hand and they broke easily. Some unknown genius solved the messiness by winding string around the entire length of the stick and unwrapping it as the graphite wore down. The brittleness problem was solved in 1761 by Kaspar Faber, a Bavarian craftsman and part-time chemist, who mixed powdered graphite with sulfur, antimony and resins, and molded the resulting glop into sticks that, when pounded into shape, hung together much better than pure graphite. All the pencil needed now was a proper casing for the slender, so-called lead. (There is no true lead in pencils; while that metal does leave a mark—along with their *penicillus* the Romans used a lead disk, which they rolled along the papyrus to mark a black line to guide their writing—it has always been too scarce, hard to refine and expensive to be adapted into a writing instrument).

In 1790 Napoleon Bonaparte was upset to find that the war he had launched to overrun Europe was depriving him of one of his favorite gadgets from Germany and England: graphite pencils. In fact, the French bureaucracy, and the

Napoleonic war machine itself, had come to depend heavily on the pencil. Nicolas Jacques Conté, a leading French chemist and inventor, was ordered to take whatever French graphite could be found and begin turning out pencils. Whether inspired by fear of failure or by the prospect of great reward, Conté hit the jackpot.

To meager French supplies of inferior graphite, he added clay as an extender, and fired the mix in a kiln. Everything adhered better than anyone had dreamed possible. The baking process turned the mix into the world's marking stick— one that stood up under reasonably rough usage. Moreover, by controlling the amount of clay mixed with the graphite, he could produce his "lead" in gradations from hard to soft, which made lines ranging from light to heavy black.

Then came the War of 1812, which cut America off from its British supply of pencils. No matter what it was mixed with, inferior U.S. graphite just wouldn't hold firm inside the rough-hewn wooden casings then used.

Now William Monroe, a Concord, Mass., cabinetmaker and tinkerer of pure Yankee strain, became the man of the moment. In his shop he made machinery which could turn out standardized, narrow wooden slats about six or seven inches long. Each slat was meticulously machine-grooved along its entire length to precisely half the thickness of a slender cylinder of molded graphite. Monroe then glued the two sections of grooved, tight-fitting wood around the graphite. And there it was—the first modern pencil! Cheap, convenient, marvelously portable, this new tool was quickly embraced by the army of clerks, artisans and managers spawned by the Industrial Revolution. Goose quill and ink became second banana.

The standard seven-inch pencil turned out today can draw a line 35 miles long, write at least 45,000 words, and survive 17 sharpenings down to a two-inch butt. It is usually attached, with a brass-colored metal ferrule, to a small nubbin of rubber mixed with pumice for erasing power. Yellow is the favorite color for the casing. Manufacturers have tried other colors—green, black, blue—but these have never sold as well.

One pencil maker ran a test stunt. He supplied a large user with 500 yellow pencils and 500 green ones. Within weeks there came complaints about the greens: The points broke too easily. They were difficult to sharpen. They were scratchy. Or they smudged. But the pencils were identical, except for the color!

The modern pencil is made of some 40 different materials. The best graphite comes from Sri Lanka, Madagascar and Mexico, the best clay from Germany. Rubber for the eraser tips comes from Malaysia, wax from Brazil. Egg-size flint pebbles, used in the tumbling machines which mix the graphite and clay, come from Belgian and Danish beaches.

Virtually all the wood used for pencil casings comes from the 200-year-old California aromatic-incense cedar, found mainly in the High Sierra. Its wood has a straight grain, uniform texture and relative softness which make it ideal not only for precision sawing but for staining and waxing, and for sharpening. The cedar logs are squared (three inches by three inches) and dried. Then they are cut again into slats five millimeters thick—half the thickness of a pencil—70 wide and 185 long. These slats are stained and waxed, then shipped to pencil manufacturers—ready to be grooved, inserted with graphite and glued together.

In this way, more than 300 different kinds of pencils are produced—including one that surgeons use to outline the operating field on a patient's skin. As someone once said, *"Everything* begins with a pencil, whether it's the design of a couturier's gown, a battleship, a baseball glove or a nuclear theory." Indeed, the common, ordinary pencil just may be the most underrated, overlooked intellectual tool in the history of mankind. Right up there next to the human brain.

Long Live The Book!

BY ERNEST O. HAUSER

What is a book? Part matter and part spirit; part thing and part thought—however you look at it, it defies definition. Its outward form, essentially unchanged in nearly 2000 years, is a design as functional as, say, the pencil or the glove; you can't improve on it. Yet, by its nature, the book is loftier than the common objects of this world. It is a vehicle of learning and enlightenment, an open sesame to countless joys and sorrows. At a touch, our book springs open, and we slip into a silent world—to visit foreign shores, to discover hidden treasure, to soar among the stars.

In 1971, by a unanimous decision of its 128 member nations, the United Nations Educational, Scientific and Cultural Organization (UNESCO) designated 1972 as the first International Book Year. The fact that the ensuing salutes were worldwide was only too appropriate, for the book is the end product of a unique conjunction of endeavors, made independently in far-flung corners of the globe. It is as if all mankind had conspired to create it.

The Chinese gave us paper. Phoenicia brought forth our alphabet. To Rome we owe the format of the book; to Germany, the art of printing from movable type. Britain and the United States perfected book production. Today, 15,000 finished books roll off high-speed presses in just one hour, and we find it hard to visualize the bookless world of our forebears, hard to imagine the enormous effort that lies behind the saga of the book.

In the beginning, there was only the spoken word. Then, to entrust his thoughts to a more lasting medium than mere memory, man took to drawing pictures representing things. Perhaps the oldest picture-script originated some 6000 years ago in Mesopotamia. Its images—bird, ox, ear of barley— were scratched into soft clay tablets, then baked hard for preservation.

But such writing was a cumbersome affair, mainly used for priestly documents and public records. What "literature" there was—such as heroic poems—depended almost totally on word-of-mouth transmission. The quick Mediterranean mind, awakening to a new culture, demanded a better way of harnessing the spoken language. Shortly before the 9th century B.C., the Phoenicians—swift seafarers, sharp traders and good record-keepers—began breaking spoken sounds into their basic elements, and shuffling the resulting "letters" to form words. I can recall the thrill I felt when, wandering among the ruins of the Phoenician port of Byblos—now in Lebanon—I saw the rudimentary inscription, hewn into the rock wall of a royal grave shaft, which stands as the world's oldest alphabetic writing. Soon the alphabet was seized upon by the Greeks, who gave letters more convenient shapes and added the still missing vowels.

No sooner had man taught himself to spell than a new problem raised its head. What to write on? Leather, tree bark, leaves and wax tablets had all proved unsatisfactory. In Egypt, for some 2500 years before Year One, texts had been inscribed on brittle sheets made from the pith of a Nile Delta water plant, papyrus. The use of this material gradually spread through the Mediterranean world. Usually, several papyrus sheets were glued together to form a scroll that could accommodate a lengthy text. (One 135-foot scroll containing the picture-script account of the deeds of Pharaoh

Ramses III is still extant.) But what a clumsy thing to read! The scroll, wrapped around a wooden stick, had to be held in the right hand, while the left slowly unwound it to reveal the next column of writing. Nevertheless, the royal library at Alexandria—destroyed in the 4th century B.C. by some unknown catastrophe or act of war—is believed to have had no fewer than 700,000 scrolls.

Relatively fragile, papyrus invited rivalry. In wealthy Pergamum, on the coast of Asia Minor, scribes wrote on specially prepared sheep, goat or calf skins. This fine, pellucid stationery, tougher than papyrus and foldable, came to be known as parchment. Shortly after Year One, an unknown Roman scribe with a sense of compactness took a stack of thin parchment sheets, folded them, and fastened them together at the spine. Thus, the book was born. Likely as not, its earliest promoters were Rome's Christians. To them, it was essential to preserve the Scriptures in the most lasting medium—and parchment didn't wilt when handled. Moreover, when one wanted to hunt up a reference, chapter and verse, a book was a lot handier than a scroll.

So it came about that, all through Europe's Dark Ages, an army of devoted monks, ensconced behind monastery walls, hand-copied the torn and shredded writings of the past on sturdy parchment sheets. Without their toil, the literary glories of ancient Greece and Rome, along with vital texts that shaped the Christian faith, might have been lost forever. It frequently took years to finish copying a thick tome, and many a sore-eyed monk, before putting away his goose quill, penned a sigh of relief on the final page: "Thank God I have finished!"

Meanwhile, in distant China, tradition has it that a gentleman named Ts'ai Lun, vexed at the wasteful use of costly silk as a writing material, reported to Emperor Ho-ti that a far cheaper substance could be made by pounding rags, tree bark and old fishing nets into a pulp, skimming thin layers off the top, and drying them. Thus, in the year 105 A.D., paper enters our story—to remain, for six centuries, a closely guarded secret of the East. It wasn't until some Chinese papermakers were captured by marauding Arabs that the pliant, blossom-white, enduring marvel took the world by storm.

The Occident saw the next major breakthrough. In 1439, a stubbornly determined German craftsman, Johann Gutenberg, began experimenting with a substitute for handwriting. If he could cast the letters of the alphabet in reusable metal type, then arrange them, in a mirror pattern, into words, lines and columns on an even-surfaced plate, an imprint taken from this plate would make one page. In place of one painstakingly handwritten book, he would be able to run off on his "press" as many imprinted books—exact copies of each other—as he wished.

Laboriously, Gutenberg put together his first page plates, each one composed of more than 3700 signs and letters. With the help of a hand-worked wooden press that he had adapted from the wine press of his native Rhineland (and which remained unchanged for the next 350 years), he started printing in a rented workshop in Mainz. It took three years to turn out some 190 copies of the Gutenberg Bible of 1455. (Today 47 copies still survive, 14 of which are in the United States. One of the finest, worth an estimated $3 million to $10 million, is on display in the Library of Congress.)

With Gutenberg's remarkable invention, book prices dropped 80 percent overnight, and learning to read became worthwhile. A mere half-century after Gutenberg's exploit, every major European country except Russia was printing its own books. It was as if floodgates had been opened. Some 520,000 titles were published in the 16th century, 1.25 million in the 17th, two million in the 18th and eight million in the 19th. Today, more than 500,000 titles come off the presses in a single year, adding up to an estimated seven *billion* individual books.

These eye-popping figures to the contrary, there are those today who predict the disappearance of the reading habit. Canadian professor and commentator Marshall McLuhan, for one, has argued that mass media—films, radio, television—involve us more completely, and hence impart their message more directly, than the familiar lineup of black letters on the printed page.

Be this as it may, the book has shown considerable fighting spirit in the face of the new threats. Book-club business has erupted into a stampede, and paperbacks are bought off store shelves as fast as they are put there. Indeed, exposure to the electronic media seems to have created a new desire to "curl up with a good book." And, as we turn its pages at our convenience, going back in leisurely fashion over a passage we've especially enjoyed, or skipping a little here, a little there, we are "involved" more intimately and completely than we could be with any other medium yet invented.

Man's thoughts and dreams, his knowledge and his aspirations, are stored in books—wealth to be tapped by all who so desire. From the first wobbly picture-script to quicker-than-the-eye offset presses, the book has come a long, arduous way, propelled by the genius and persistence of many individuals and nations. Indeed, all humanity has reason to be proud of the book, for it shows us at our very best. Long live the book!

Word Power Test No. 23

The Joy of Self-Improvement

BY PETER FUNK

In a recent jubilant letter, a reader wrote that he had been going over the word tests in 30 back issues of the *Digest*, to prepare for a scholarship test. It worked! He scored outstandingly well on the vocabulary-based test, and got the scholarship. Building a more powerful vocabulary can benefit you as well. Begin with the words below, which have appeared in *Digest* articles. Choose the word *nearest in meaning* to the key word. Answers appear at the end of this test.

1. **aspire** (ă spīr′)—A: to end. B: animate. C: dream. D: aim for.
2. **sonar**—apparatus to A: detect something in the air. B: locate objects under water. C: measure rain. D: anticipate earthquakes.
3. **cosset** (kŏs′ it)—A: to bind. B: encourage. C: pamper. D: protect.
4. **precipitate** (pre sip′ ĭ tāt)—A: to obscure. B: cause to separate. C: weaken. D: flirt.
5. **egalitarian** (ē gal ĭ tair′ ē an)—A: gallant. B: democratic. C: French-style. D: dignified.
6. **substantive** (sub′ stan tĭv)—A: practical. B: essential. C: successive. D: replaceable.
7. **indomitable** (in dŏm′ ĭ tuh b'l)—A: meek. B: unconquerable. C: tireless. D: overbearing.
8. **countervail**—A: to counterbalance. B: correct. C: argue with. D: complain.
9. **disproportionate** (dis pro por′ shun it)—A: varying. B: rarefied. C: unworkable. D: disparate.

10. **aberration** (ab ur ā′ shun)—A: deviation. B: falsehood. C: injury. D: disgrace.

11. **expertise** (ex per tēz′)—A: flexibility. B: fussiness. C: skill. D: ease.

12. **accentuate** (ak sen′ chōō āt)—A: to indicate. B: specify. C: affect. D: emphasize.

13. **cadge** (kaj)—A: to enclose. B: track. C: trick. D: beg.

14. **motivation** (mō tǐ vā′ shun)—A: incentive. B: obstacle. C: ambition. D: tendency.

15. **regenerate** (re jěn′ ě rāt)—A: to re-create. B: make younger. C: supplant. D: sanctify.

16. **acrid** (ak′ rid)—A: dry. B: painful. C: nauseating. D: pungent.

17. **chagrin** (shah grin′)—A: mockery. B: disgust. C: annoyance. D: unpleasantness.

18. **progeny** (prǒj′ ě nē)—A: a genius. B: offspring. C: growth. D: unpleasantness.

19. **empirical** (em pǐr′ ǐ k'l)—A: based on experience. B: having visions of power. C: proud and disdainful. D: relying on theory.

20. **obelisk** (ŏb′ uh lisk)—A: archaic word. B: ancient riddle. C: pagoda. D: stone pillar.

ANSWERS

1. **aspire**—D: To aim for, in the sense of striving toward excellence. Latin *aspirare* (to breathe upon).

2. **sonar**—B: An apparatus that locates underwater objects by sending out high-frequency sound waves. An acronym from SO(und) N(avigation) A(nd) R(anging).

3. **cosset**—C: To pamper; coddle. English dialectal *cosset* (pet lamb).

4. **precipitate**—B: To cause a partially soluble substance to be separated out from a liquid and deposited in solid form. Latin *praecipitare* (cast headlong). "Seawater *precipitates* minerals across the ocean floor."

5. **egalitarian**—B: Democratic; advocating equal political, economic, social and legal rights for everyone. French *égalité* (equality).

6. **substantive**—B: Relating to what is essential; directly bearing on a matter; as, a *substantive* argument. Old French *substantif* (self-existent).

7. **indomitable**—B: Unconquerable; persevering; refusing to be overcome by difficulties. Latin *indomitabilis* (untamable).

8. **countervail**—A: To counterbalance; offset; as, the *countervailing* effect of a new weapons system. Old French *contrevaloir*.

9. **disproportionate**—D: Disparate; out of proportion with regard to size, form, value or number. From *dis* (reverse of) and *proportion*.

10. **aberration**—A: Deviation; departure from whatever is ordinary or normal. Latin *aberrare* (wander; go astray).

11. **expertise**—C: Skill; expert knowledge; know-how. French.

12. **accentuate**—D: To emphasize; stress. When someone *accentuates* the positive, he heightens, sharpens or intensifies the non-negative aspects. Latin *accentus* (accent).

13. **cadge**—A: To beg; sponge; as, to *cadge* money. Possibly from Middle English *cadger* (peddler).

14. **motivation**—A: Incentive; inducement or a stimulation. "His *motivation* is the simple desire to be rich." Latin *motivus* (serving to move).

15. **regenerate**—A: To re-create by new growth; as, "Each year the stag *regenerates* its molted horns." Also, to cause to be spiritually reborn. Latin *regenerare* (to reproduce).

16. **acrid**—D: An *acrid* taste or smell is pungent, sharp, irritating. Latin *acer* (sharp, cutting).

17. **chagrin**—C: Annoyance or vexation caused by a failure, disappointment or humiliating incident. "With *chagrin* she realized her mistake." Old French *graignier* (to sorrow).

18. **progeny**—B: Offspring; descendants; as, "All the old man's *progeny* were interested in his will. Old French *progenie*, from Latin.

19. **empirical**—A: Based on direct or practical experience rather than theory. From Greek *Empirici*, an ancient association of physicians who treated illness pragmatically.

20. **obelisk**—D: Four-sided, tapering stone pillar with a pyramid-like top. "The Washington Monument is an *obelisk*." Greek *obeliskos*.

VOCABULARY RATINGS

20—19 correct ....exceptional
18—15 correct ....excellent
14—12 correct ....good

Words That Have Appeared In These Tests

Four Entertaining, Informative Books From America's Most Trusted Magazine
READER'S DIGEST

DRAMA IN REAL LIFE
04723-7/$2.50 _____

contains stories of endurance, ingenuity and incredible bravery that take place among real people in unexpected situations.

THE LIVING WORLD OF NATURE
04720-2/$2.50 _____

explores the marvels and mysteries of earth, sea and sky in a collection of distinguished essays by nature specialists.

UNFORGETTABLE CHARACTERS
04722-9/$2.50 _____

is drawn from the highly popular "The Most Unforgettable Character I Ever Met" series, featuring short, amusing tales of both the famous and the obscure.

WORD POWER
04721-0/$2.50 _____

is a fascinating anthology of tests from "It Pays to Enrich Your Word Power," with articles by such language experts as Clifton Fadiman, Edwin Newman and Vance Packard.

Berkley/Reader's Digest Books

Available at your local bookstore or return this form to:
Berkley Book Mailing Service
P.O. Box 690
Rockville Centre. NY 11570

Please send me the above titles. I am enclosing $_____
(Please add 75¢ per copy to cover postage and handling). Send check or money order—no cash or C.O.D.'s. Allow six weeks for delivery.

NAME_____

ADDRESS_____

CITY_____ STATE/ZIP_____ 82